The Rookie Recipient

Our True Love Story Beyond the Viral Video

Heather & Steve Winfree

The Rookie Recipient
Our True Love Story Beyond the Viral Video

Authors: Heather & Steve Winfree
Contributing Editor: Brenda E. Cortez
Contributing Editor/Proofreader: Lyda Rose Haerle
Cover Design: Heather Winfree
Cover Design, Layout: Michael Nicloy
Cover Photograph: Vanderbilt Media Relations
Interior Layout: Griffin Mill

Interior images courtesy of Heather and Steve Winfree

ISBN-13: 978-1-957351-52-0

PUBLISHED BY NICO 11 PUBLISHING & DESIGN
MUKWONAGO, WISCONSIN
Michael Nicloy, Publisher
www.nico11publishing.com

Be well read.

Quantity and wholesale order
requests may be emailed to:

mike@nico11publishing.com
or be made by phone: 217.779.9677

Printed in The United States of America

This book is dedicated to everyone who, like us, has struggled but continues to persevere. True heroes are not only those who save lives, but also those who refuse to give up on life.

– Heather Winfree

To every nurse, housekeeper, food service worker, and doctor whose dedication and hard work made my journey bearable. You all are, amongst my wife, my heroes.

– Steve Winfree

To our son, Levi - your presence has been both motivating and distracting during the writing of this book. We love you so much!

– Mom and Dad

ACT ONE

Chapter 01

By Heather

NEXT OF KIN

It hurt to breathe. Up until that moment, I had no idea grief could manifest itself physically. Before, I had always thought of grief as just an intense sadness, an ache, but as I was truly feeling it for the first time, I realized how sharp, real, painful, and exhausting grief could be. Grief is crushing. It felt like there was an anvil on my chest. I clutched my chest as I strained to take in every breath as if I were swallowing hardening cement.

It was as if my body knew it was not right for me to keep on breathing and living, not without him, not without my other half. We had just recently celebrated our fifth wedding anniversary. I was only twenty-six years old; we were supposed to have our whole lives before us. We were supposed to grow old together. In an instant, everything was changing. My husband, Steve, had battled kidney disease since he was 18 years old. Slowly, over the years, his kidney function had continued to decline. His kidneys were barely doing their job anymore, so Steve began dialysis the month before this horrific incident that I will detail below. At just 31 years old, he was a noticeably young dialysis patient. Twice a week, he went to a dialysis center to have his blood cleaned of all the toxins his body was unable to filter out. He had a dialysis catheter port in his chest, which they used to hook the machine up to. Steve went to dialysis earlier that day and then came home to nap. It was not uncommon for him to be exhausted after dialysis and for him to go straight to the bedroom when he got home. We did not know it at the time, but his port had become infected that day, and he was going into septic shock.

He called me into the bedroom with a weak cry and alerted me that he did not feel good. I felt his forehead, and he was burning up. I rushed to the medicine cabinet to grab the thermometer to take his temperature. I became even more alarmed as the number 105 stared back at me. He was starting to go delirious, slurring his words, and his eyes were glazed over. It was evident something was very wrong. I helped him out of the bed and positioned myself under his arm to be a crutch for him, and then I rushed him to the hospital. He was taken back immediately, and before long, they told me he was declining fast and would need to be transferred to the intensive care unit (ICU). Doctors, nurses, and the staff were moving so fast around me that I did not have time to process what was happening…until I was left alone in the ICU waiting room.

It felt like hours, but I am sure it was most likely only minutes. My thoughts were scrambled, and I shook with fear. When the receptionist returned from her break, she looked at her chart, looked at me, and called me to her desk. She asked, "Are you Steve's next of kin?" For some reason, when she said that, I felt as if she was already referring to me as his widow. I wanted to scream, "NO, I am his wife!! I am Steve's wife!" *Next of kin* sounded so impersonal, so cold, and so lifeless. It hit me right then that this was way more serious than I had thought. We had just gone to the movies last night, and now, today, my husband was dying. I was the next of kin, the one responsible for medical decisions since my husband was not coherent. The receptionist checked me in and told me to have a seat. She would let me know when I could go back to see him.

Sitting in the waiting room, I began to process what was happening. My world came crashing down as I pieced together things the doctors said earlier around me. How could I come to terms with the fact that I was losing him, my best friend, my soulmate, the love of my life? The thought of my life going on without him was unbearable. Hot, stinging tears welled up in my eyes, but I choked them back as I sat and waited. If I allowed myself to cry, it would be like admitting that this was real. *This could not possibly be real. Nope, it must be a nightmare.*

The world around me narrowed, and my peripheral vision blurred. I could only focus on one object at a time. I looked at the clock on the wall, a chair, and the receptionist's desk, but they didn't have meaning. Nothing made sense. What was happening? People seemed to tiptoe around me because it was too hard to explain what was going on. I swallowed the tears and the lump in my throat, along with the grief, but I only felt worse the more I tried to suppress it, making it even more laborious to breathe. I began whispering to myself, "Breathe, breathe, breathe," as I inhaled through my nose and exhaled out my mouth. Reminding myself to continue doing this automatic function felt necessary because, in all honesty, I did not want to breathe anymore. Not without my husband by my side. As I continued to whisper to myself to breathe, I put my head in my hands and leaned over in my chair until my head was between my knees. The thought that I most likely would be leaving this hospital without my husband was the most terrifying realization. I was crumbling. My whispers, reminding me to continue to force myself to keep breathing, were interrupted when the receptionist sympathetically stated, "You can go back now."

I jumped up so fast that my head spun, and I was dizzy. She grabbed my bag and escorted me back to Steve's room in the intensive care unit. I think she somehow knew it was taking everything in me to breathe, and anything else would be too much at that moment. When we reached the room, she told me to let her know if I needed anything at all. All I needed, all I wanted, was in that room. The room was eerily quiet except for the sounds of machines attempting to keep my husband alive. He was usually the life of the room, but here he was, lying nearly lifeless on the hospital bed. The medical team had him stable for now, but the infection had spread throughout his entire body. His heart rate was so slow that they could not give him anything for the pain for fear his heart would stop. His eyes were closed, and although he was unconscious, his pain was evident from his furrowed brow.

I sat in the chair beside his bed. My best friend was there but not really. I trembled with fear, and for the first time in the seven years of our being together, my husband could not comfort me. Everything I was trying so hard to suppress came pouring out of me all at once. "Why God, why?" I screamed in my head. I sat there in anger, with grief knocking on my door, feeling sorry for myself and angry at God. I thought of all the beautiful things God was taking from me. He was stealing our future and our dreams. My husband was dying.

What in the world was I supposed to do? How could I live without him? All I wanted was more time. Then, as if a switch turned inside of me, I decided I would cherish what time, however little, we still had left. Instead of continuing the pity party I was having for myself, I would love on my husband. There would be plenty of time for grief later—an infinite, crippling amount of time; the rest of my life. Okay, I had not completely stopped feeling sorry for myself, but I crawled beside Steve in his hospital bed and looked at him with all my love. I traced his cheek with my hand, trying to memorize his face, and then I held his hand. I loved the way my hand felt in his. I never wanted to let him go. I put his arm around me and melted into his embrace with my head on his chest. I needed to savor the time if this was all we had left. I let myself sink in and drown in this moment.

My eyes closed as I tried to memorize how it felt to be in his arms. Then, without even thinking, I began to sing. In a whispered tone, I sang the lyrics to our wedding song into his chest. My tears poured down onto his hospital gown as memories flooded back to me. I pictured in my mind the first time we danced to that song while we were dating in his apartment at college. Part of the words to the song are "whatever comes our way, ah we'll see it through, and you know that's what our love can do." I believed those words as they left my lips in song, despite how hopeless things felt at that moment. It didn't matter we were in a dark and cold room, and it didn't matter what the doctors believed. I knew if anyone's love could see them through near death, it was our love. I hoped that Steve, in his unconscious state, somehow heard my song and then felt the lyrics in his heart. He needed to believe it, too, so he would keep on fighting for us.

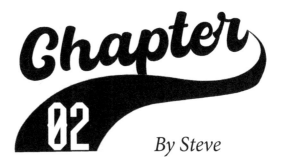

JUST A BOY, A BALL, AND A LAUNDRY BASKET

1989-2003

Imagine a four-year-old running around with a small bouncy ball and a makeshift basketball hoop, also known as a laundry basket, shooting for hours. This was me as a little boy, and I had become obsessed with the sport of basketball at an incredibly early age. My dad had played basketball at a small town in East Tennessee called Harriman, and he would tell me the greatest stories about his days playing. At that young age, it appeared to me that my dad was the best basketball player on earth!

Growing up, my dad played ball with me all the time, whether it be throwing a soft stuffed football we had, a baseball, or, of course, a basketball. I remember his telling me the devastating story of how he was on track to play high-level college basketball, but during his senior year in high school, he tore his ACL. Back then, a torn ACL was a career-ender, and unfortunately, that rang painfully true for him. My dad was so close to being a college basketball player, and it always made me sad that he did not get to play. He always told me that as a father, you always want to see your kids do better and go further than you did. At the time, I thought he meant basketball, which very well could have been a part of it, but as I became an adult, I realized he meant much more.

Hearing those words made me obsessed with making my dad proud, and all I wanted was to hear him say I did well and that he was proud of me. I always wanted to hear his praises after a basketball game, but he reminded me he also meant in school as well. It worked because that drive led me to earn all A's and B's as a student, and I scored a perfect score on my math standardized test in sixth grade. Due to that perfect score, I was invited to take the ACT through Duke University as an incoming seventh grader. As you'll read, I did not end up going to Duke.

Even though basketball was the sport I excelled in, my love for baseball was even greater. I loved playing baseball in the backyard with my little brother, Chris, and we stayed out there all day in the summers. We went to Atlanta Braves games and Cincinnati Reds games as a family. I was obsessed with getting to the field early to watch batting practice and catch a glimpse of the famous players I had in my baseball card collection. I loved collecting cards of Ken Griffey, Jr., Frank Thomas, Juan Gonzales, Cal Ripken, Jr., and every player on the Braves. The summer smells at the ballpark left me in awe of the magical experience. Just something about baseball captured my heart, and I will always regret not playing in high school. Although sports were a large part of my childhood, they were not my only aspirations in life.

Growing up, I loved pretending to be characters, and I would write scenes and act them out while alone in my room. Our family loved watching movies together, and I will never forget the impact I felt when my dad played the movie, *Slam Dunk Ernest*. My eyes lit up with fascination as my dad told me the actor playing the janitor was from Knoxville. If a guy from Knoxville achieved my dream of acting, I knew it was possible for me, too. The actor who showed me dreams can come true is Cylk Cozart. My idol appeared in an array of movies, including *Conspiracy Theory*, *Blue Chips*, *Eraser* with Arnold Schwarzenegger, and also popular television shows such as *Saved by the Bell*, and my favorite, *Fresh Prince of Belair* in which he played Hank Farley, who dated the character played by Tyra Banks. I envisioned myself as an actor, just like him, and I dreamed of meeting him in person one day. Years later, I ended up seeing him in person at a celebrity basketball game, but I was too intimidated to approach him.

I did not share my dreams of being a writer and actor with my family and friends. Instead, I focused on basketball because I enjoyed it and needed the bond it created with my dad. My mom would even come out and shoot sometimes, and I quickly realized I inherited my athleticism from my dad and my sense of humor from my mom. When I got a little older, my parents got me involved in travel league basketball and summer camps, and they made sure at least one of them was always at my game. As an adult now, I see how amazing that was. As a young athlete, I was voted the best player in my league, which I attribute to all of the time I spent as a four-year-old shooting a ball into a box or laundry basket.

I recall times as a kid running around but feeling weird in my stomach and having a sudden urge to want to eat. I became a hungry beast and was not sure where it came from. My parents took me to the doctor a few times because I was extremely skinny and constantly drinking water, which are signs of diabetes. Each time, they were told I did not have diabetes, or perhaps I was borderline, but nothing suggested I had it.

By the time I was nearing the end of high school, I had grown to be six-foot-two, was a sharpshooter, and could jump and dunk quite easily. One of my best memories was when I got to dunk against our main rivals, Clinton, and our student section went nuts, chanting my nickname.

As a high school senior, I began receiving college letters, and I will never forget my first one from Webster University in Saint Louis. My heart was filled with joy when I came home and read it, and I remember crying as I thought I could play college ball and make my dad proud. My goal was to make it this far since that was his goal for me because he didn't have the opportunity due to his injury. I was so close to achieving that, which made me happier than any son you could imagine.

Around my eighteenth birthday, I committed to Maryville College, an NCAA Division 3 college about 45 minutes away from home, just outside of Knoxville, Tennessee. Over the summer, I attended many practice sessions and played in scrimmages, giving me a good feel for the college basketball pace. It was much quicker than high school. I remember a time in the weight room when I was alone and staring at the NCAA logo in big letters in the mirror. My emotions took over and brought me straight back to memories of being a little boy running around in my underwear at the age of four and five, shooting relentlessly. I had made it. I accomplished my goal of playing NCAA basketball, and I knew I would make my dad proud.

Chapter 03

By Heather

I WANT TO BE A MOM!

Growing up, I was the third child in a family of four children, but I have always considered myself the *middle* child because my older siblings were each the first-born boy and the first-born girl, and my little sister was the baby in the family. I never felt like I belonged in this loud Italian family since I was meek, unsure of myself, and indecisive. Despite my insecurities, one thing I was always sure of, as far back as I can remember, was my answer to the question, "What do you want to be when you grow up?" My response has always been confident and unequivocally strong – "I want to be a mom!"

These feelings began when I was just a toddler myself. I wanted a baby of my own, and I did get one. My younger sister, Sarah, was two years younger than me and was "my baby." Of course, I had dolls to play with, but I also got to experience a real baby with my younger sister. People often mistook us for twins; we grew up as best friends. My family attended church regularly, and I remember praying a lot as a child. My most frequent prayer was for my bedroom to magically clean itself. I closed my eyes and prayed to God as if I were making a wish to a genie in a lamp. I never received those desired results, but I continued to pray for a clean room. Every time I opened my eyes to the disappointment of my messy room, I shrugged. My other frequent prayer request that I prayed from an incredibly young age was for "another baby." I remember my mother telling my siblings that she was expecting a baby. I was thrilled! We would have another baby for me to adore and play with. God had heard my prayers and answered this prayer, unlike the prayer for a magically clean room. I was going to get *my baby*. Not long after that announcement, my mother called us into the living room for a family meeting, and she cried as she told us she lost the baby.

I kept praying, and eventually, my mother announced again that she was expecting. I was too young to understand the mechanics of making a baby at the time. I didn't know my parents were actively trying for another child, so in my naïve mind, I felt as if my prayers were solely responsible for her pregnancies. The heartbreak continued when, just like before, she broke the same devastating news to us again. She miscarried again. Seeing the devastation that another loss had on my mother, I stopped praying for another sibling. I felt guilty; I felt like I was the cause of her pain, even though it was not my fault. My heart ached. Mom lost both babies at a point too early to determine the gender, but I believed they were both baby girls. I named them and thought of them often.

I do not recall the age I was then. To be honest, I have blocked out a lot of my childhood. If I had to guess, I would say I was around eight or so. All I remember is the arm of the cream-colored formal living room sofa with a red floral pattern that I clung to at that moment for comfort, and the flowers and leaves that I traced sullenly through blurry, tear-filled eyes. I watched those tears periodically kerplunk onto that sofa as I listened to devastating news. This is the room where we had "family meetings."

This was not our family room with the comfy broken-in couch where we had friends over for parties, pretended to be the perfect happy family, and had movie nights with popcorn. This was the formal living area where only serious "family meetings" occurred, which in our house meant bad news. Did other families have formal rooms where seemingly only bad news occurred?

There was no popcorn to be found hidden between these sofa cushions. Two matching cream-colored floral couches faced each other, with a wooden coffee table between them, and two matching formal upholstered chairs in two corners of the room. An uncomfortable room strictly for uncomfortable conversations. This is where my mother told me she lost her babies…my baby siblings, then a string of uncomfortable conversations starting in my early teens where she told us my father left, followed by her telling us they were trying a legal separation, then where she said he was coming back, but only to evacuate with us during an approaching hurricane. Then, on that cold-hearted couch, my mom shared they were divorcing, and while the ink was still drying on their divorce papers, another bomb dropped. My mom, my sisters, and I would be moving from Florida to Tennessee (my older brother was in college at this point). There I sat, vulnerable and highly emotional at the age of sixteen, and the only way of life I knew had just vanished in a puff of smoke.

Years of tears are soaked into the fabric of that unpleasant couch where I received all my childhood life-altering news. The loss of my siblings, then my family as I knew it, and finally, my friendships, my city, my home, and everything that was familiar. I clung to that cream-colored arm when everything around me was falling apart.

The next time I would pray for a baby, it would be for *my* baby.

I never imagined how hard my journey to motherhood would be. A few months before Steve and I met in college, I was diagnosed with polycystic ovarian syndrome (PCOS). This condition can cause fertility issues, among other symptoms, such as weight gain, abnormal menstruation, heavy or absent periods, acne, hair loss, and unwanted hair growth. For me, PCOS presented with heavy and very painful periods. I did not know it at the time, but my body was also suffering from endometriosis, another condition that can cause painful, irregular periods and infertility. I saw the gynecologist several times during my sophomore year of college due to excruciating pain near what I suspected was my right ovary. The doctor examined me multiple times and ordered ultrasounds, but the results revealed nothing. My doctor grew tired of my complaints of an ailment she believed only existed in my head. I remember being told quite sternly, "It is all in your head, Heather. We don't see anything on your ultrasounds. There is nothing wrong with you!" I left that appointment mentally defeated because I knew my body and the relentless pain meant something was wrong. After my efforts to advocate for myself failed, I decided not to bring it up again. Ten years later, and still suffering in pain, I finally dared to talk about my unacknowledged suffering with another doctor.

By Steve

I AM SORRY TO INFORM YOU...

Off to College

My first semester of college began, and I adjusted to life as a college athlete away from my parents for the first time. My classes were harder than I expected, and constantly thinking about my girlfriend and basketball, at the time, did not help. These things had me preoccupied, which meant less time for my studies. I wasn't failing, but I expected more of myself. The newfound freedom of being away from home can be intoxicating for any college freshman. I was not into drinking and never touched a drug, but I prioritized the things I enjoyed over my studying.

We were three weeks away from our first game, my first game as a college basketball player, and the official running through the ribbon to celebrate accomplishing my dad's goal of his son doing better than he did. All we needed were our preseason physicals, which I wasn't worried about in the least. My eye was on the first game and getting started on this new journey I had been working so hard for. I arrived at the gym and headed to the back hallway for my physical. They took my blood pressure and pulse, and then the not-so-fun "turn and cough," which everyone had a good laugh with. The doctor was a bit rough with exam tactics, which reminded me of the scene from *Friends* when Chandler came home from the tailor Joey had recommended to him.

My final hurdle of the physical exam was the blood pressure cuff, and I would be off and running. My readings kept coming back extremely high, with numbers around 180 over 130. It did not make sense because I was 18, weighed 175 pounds, and felt great. Because of the high readings, they referred me to my family doctor for a more complete check-up. I had not given the pre-season physical exam any thought whatsoever, and I was a bit irritated because I felt fine. My focus as a freshman in college was playing ball and having fun.

I went and had my blood drawn at our family doctor. They said my results would be back shortly, and they would call me if any irregularities showed up. I headed back to campus to prepare for the first big game. My heart raced with excitement and gratitude. While in my dorm room working on homework, I received a phone call from a number I did not recognize, but I answered anyway. My heart sank, but I had no idea what they had just told me. My BUN and creatinine numbers were elevated, and they referred me to a nephrologist. *What?*

I continued with my homework and then received another call to schedule an appointment to see the special doctor, starting with an "N." My parents were set to come with me to what I thought was just a regular appointment. Oh, boy! How wrong I was. I can still envision it to this day. My nerves started jumping as we waited for the doctor to come in. I stared at the blood pressure cuff, and all feeling left my body instantly as I couldn't turn away from the cuff. Then I heard a voice outside of the door and a quick two-knock.

"I am sorry to inform you that you have kidney disease. Your kidney function is at less than 50%," the nephrologist told me. I had no idea what this doctor was talking about. My college basketball career had just begun, and all I could think about was returning to campus to continue my life. What other things did an eighteen-year-old college guy need to worry about besides getting ready for our first game? I don't recall reacting much to the news because I felt fine. Little did I know then how that moment changed my life forever.

As he left the room, he put his hand on my shoulder and said to me, "Son, you will be fine." He planned to talk to my head coach about my results. My mind returned to my childhood memories of playing basketball and wanting to make my dad proud.

The day of the traditional "Midnight Madness" game to kick off the season had arrived, and both the team and the town were jumping with excitement. Enthusiasm rushed through my veins as I walked to the arena for Midnight Madness. I went straight to the locker room and changed into the official game jersey for the first time. The feel of that jersey on my skin sent shivers down my spine. It was happening. I poked my head out of the locker room to peek at the stands, and there in the front row were my dad and my older brother. I could see the excitement on their faces. Butterflies fluttered around in my stomach with the anticipation of lining up for our grand entrance onto the court. The crowd was standing and ready to cheer on this year's team.

My emotional high was interrupted when my head coach yelled, "*Hey, Winfree, I want to talk to you back in my office.*" I will never forget my walk of shame as I left his office and headed back towards my teammates. They were hyped and motioning for me to join them in line, but instead, I walked right by them and straight to my dad and brother in the stands. As I got closer, my knees shook, and an uneasy feeling consumed my body. I stopped and said, "*Dad, I am so sorry, but I will never play basketball again.*" Those words came out of my mouth, but in my mind, I was standing there as a four-year-old saying, "*Hey, Dad, I am sorry for all the times you will throw a ball with me. I am sorry for all the times you will shoot with me on the driveway. I am sorry for all of the hundreds of practices and games you will be there for, and most importantly, I am sorry for not doing better than you did and for letting you down in fourteen years, but I hope you are still proud.*"

I am certain that is not what he thought, nor would he ever make me feel like a failure because of something beyond my control, but those were the feelings I put on myself because I wanted to make him proud and achieve a goal that I had fought so hard for. My demons of failure and worthlessness took over when the thought of never playing basketball was all I could see. The dreams I had were crushed and stomped on and out of my life forever, or so I thought.

Living a life that didn't include basketball tore me apart, so I decided to transfer to the University of Tennessee after that first semester. Steve, the basketball player, no longer existed. My identity was gone in an instant. If you've ever played organized sports, I'm sure you can relate to my feelings when it all came to a screeching halt. You dedicate so much time to practicing, working out, and doing all it takes to be your best that it becomes your world. You grieve the lifestyle you lived and enjoyed, especially when you didn't expect it to end when it did.

Fall 2004

Even though I couldn't play basketball as planned, I still enjoyed the game in a league at the student recreation center on campus. Then, an opportunity arose to possibly be a practice player for Coach Summitt and the Lady Vols basketball team.

Coach Summitt was legendary, so why not ask about being a practice player? She invited me to try out for the practice squad, and I made it! That meant attending practice every day against the Lady Vols basketball team. It didn't compare to being a collegiate basketball player, but I was honored to be a part of it. Plus, I had a good time suiting up at the arena I dreamed of playing in as a kid. I had always imagined hitting a three-pointer and hearing the band go into the song "Rocky Top." The coaching staff knew of my health issues and assured me proper breaks and access to all the team's resources including doctors and trainers. They promised they would not allow me to exert myself in a way that would be harmful to my overall health.

Coach Summitt taught me so much about being tough and persevering even when life seemed impossible. That guidance couldn't have come at a better time. She knew my story, which may have had something to do with me making the team, but I never asked. It didn't matter because I had found myself learning about life from a legend in the form of basketball. Being on the practice team also taught me a lot about my abilities as a basketball player…those girls made me look silly. I remember they once instructed me to guard a redshirt Freshman, Candace Parker. She was considered the best female basketball player to ever come out of high school.

I remember the first practice when I got yelled at by Coach Summitt. We were doing a defensive drill for the ladies called "The Shell." The Lady Vols would show their defensive positioning based on where the ball was around the arc. I had the lucky spot to play low on the block as an offensive player. Since the girls were just showing stance as the ball moved around, I figured I would lightly move around. I realized that was a huge mistake when Coach Summitt blew her whistle and asked me if I was ok and if my legs were hurting. After letting her know my appreciation for her concern, she quickly let me know I had better move the area between my lower back and legs quickly. One never forgets the first time they got the Coach Summitt yell and stare! Your body would freeze up, and life seemed to stop as the entire team looked at you to see if you would break out in tears. Fortunately, I did not cry, at least not in front of everybody. Despite her hard outer shell, Coach Summitt was also one of the most kind and selfless people you would ever meet. She was right there to pick you back up if you were injured. I experienced this side of her firsthand as well. I had been positively motivated and influenced by my time with Coach Summitt and by being a part of the Lady Vols in college. Most notably, unbeknownst to me, this would lead to a future where my pastor would introduce me as Steve, the former Lady Vol. Watching a confused Baptist's face trying to figure that one out has always been amusing, to say the least.

One of my most memorable moments of Coach Summitt was the day I tore a ligament in my knee at practice and she went with me to the training room and waited with me until my dad arrived. A week later I came back to practice for rehab and physical therapy the day after Coach Summitt became the winningest coach in college basketball history with win #880, surpassing Coach Dean Smith. Reporters were waiting for her to come out of the locker room, and she walked right by them and immediately came to check on me. She passed on an opportunity to be praised for her amazing accomplishment and instead chose to catch up with me. Her character and care for her team, practice player or not, is why I believe she is the greatest coach of all time.

Despite my love for sports, I still really wanted to be a writer, actor, and comedian. I used to write all of the time growing up and now occasionally when I found time. I had an obsession with watching stand-up comedians. The way they made me laugh pulled me away from the anxiety I was riddled with as a kid. While I enjoyed a great belly laugh, I wanted to make others laugh. Helping others smile and forget their worries sounded appealing to me. Back in my first year at the University of Tennessee, I attended an open mic night at a bar to watch stand-up for the first time. The inspiration I felt from that night led me to write some jokes of my own. I practiced with my girlfriend, who was the only person who knew about my desire to do stand-up. Looking back, I'm amazed I even wanted to do such a thing, but I returned to that bar for open mic night. There I stood, shaky knees and all, telling jokes for seven minutes in front of strangers. Initially, they had to remind me to hold the mic closer to my mouth, but I confidently delivered my jokes, letting the crowd know I was a virgin at stand-up comedy. All the laughter and clapping I received made it worth the ball of nerves I had rolling in my stomach. The feeling of seeing people laugh and tell me *good job* as I took a shot in the dark at a childhood dream of mine was indescribable. That's the kind of guy I was before my disease took over. I looked forward to trying new things as I persevered through life with a smile on my face. The only thing standing in my way back then was myself.

I graduated in Spring of 2007 with a degree in Sport Management and a minor in Business. I could not believe how fast college had gone by. Even though I had been diagnosed with kidney disease during college, I still played some basketball, went to classes, made some great friends, and graduated. Kidney disease can be a silent disease that many people don't realize they have until their kidney function is dangerously low. I knew I had it, but since I wasn't sick and led a normal life, I naïvely believed it wasn't serious and that I was in the clear from there on out.

By Steve

CAMERAS ROLLING, BACKGROUND, ACTION!

Summer of 2007

The summer of 2007 will be rooted in my memory forever. After graduating from college, I began my first post-college internship at Disney's *Wide World of Sports* in Lake Buena Vista, Florida. The other interns were great, and most of us became friends. I enjoyed living with my roommates Jason, Lorenzo, and Chris. They were all fun and unique in their own ways. Jason and I hit it off easily since we shared a very similar sense of humor. We spent each day together at the office we called *Cubicle World*. My friends AJ, Trey, Matt, Jason, Mario, and Zach were all seated in the same aisle. We had a great dynamic working together. I miss those guys! My other friends Jess, Ashleigh, Lauren, Meeghan, and my boss, Steve, made it even more fun. We all became a family that year at Disney, and they are people I will cherish for the rest of my life.

During this time at Disney, I noticed some symptoms that were derived from my kidney disease. The doctors and I believed it was turf toe soreness from being on my feet all day or possibly stress fractures, but no one thought it had to do with my failing kidneys. The joints in my toes became very painful. It felt like they were broken, but I could not recall hurting my foot. The intense pain cut like a sharp knife, then felt as though the knife was doused in gasoline and lit on fire as it stabbed my joint repeatedly. It was odd that a young guy, only 22, would be going through this without explanation.

While working for Disney Sports, a surreal opportunity practically landed in my lap. They sent me to a local high school where we were hosting one of our numerous basketball tournaments. My work day was over, but since the high school was close to where I lived, I told my boss I would be happy to go. When I arrived at the high school, I couldn't help but notice many people hanging around trailers and large racks of clothing next to cameras and large lights. It appeared I had stumbled onto a movie set, and I could not believe it! I went into the gymnasium to take care of what I came for, but since it was the end of the day for me, I decided to hang around and see if I could find a way onto the movie set. As I was finishing, they were about to film outside the gym, which was the only way in and out of our tournament. I needed to ensure the players and their families could enter the gym for the games. I saw a lady walking around with a headset on and figured she looked important, so I went over to talk to her. The nice lady answered all my questions, such as, "What is going on? Is this a movie or TV show? How can I be in the movie?" As luck would have it, she was in charge of the background workers, also known as extras. Her name was Jennifer, and she asked how old I was and if I would be off the next day. Yes! I was actually off for the next two days, so she said she would put me in the movie as an extra. Jennifer instructed me what to wear, and to come back the next morning at 6:00 a.m. Was it for real that I had just stumbled upon an actual Hollywood movie set and was invited to be in it? Check! The movie was a teen coming-of-age movie about high schoolers and mixed martial arts. That was all I knew of the production.

When I arrived the next morning, Jennifer had me sign some paperwork and told me to hang tight. She eventually led me to the set where they were shooting outside a cafeteria, and they told me to sit at one of the tables where the high schoolers would be eating in the scene. She explained pantomiming and proper set etiquette to me, such as being quiet in between takes, not looking into the camera, not using cell phones to take photos, and not making the scene about you. I soaked up every moment of the experience and tried to learn as much as possible. Some of the actors were sitting at a table close to mine. In between takes, I said hi to them, and they were friendly and said it back, but they were focused on their job. The actors were Sean Faris (*Yours, Mine, & Ours*), Evan Peters (*American Horror Story/X-Men* as Quicksilver), and Amber Heard, a young actress. Yes, the same Amber Heard who went on to marry Johnny Depp.

As the day ended, Jennifer asked me if I would be interested in returning. Of course, I said absolutely. The next shoot was set at a local high school football field and was a night shoot, so we were up all night filming this particular scene. It was "raining" during the scene, so we spent all night soaked. I wasn't expecting that, and it was a major eye-opener to what life on set can be like with long hours, difficult conditions, freezing, and having to repeat the same scene over and over. I sat in the stands for the scene, and I decided to call my brothers and my roommate Jason to join me as extras.

For the second night of shooting, my little brother and I were promoted to feature extras, and they put us on the field! We both played on the main character's team, and my brother was asked to play tight end on the field. We had a blast! That scene was the very first scene of the movie, and it led to a massive, bench-clearing brawl on the field. The production team told me to rip my helmet off once I saw the fight break out and run straight to the main character to defend him. My brother was also told to rush the field and defend the main character. They wanted him to keep his helmet on for safety reasons, but he insisted he did not travel eleven hours to be in a movie with his face covered. He did take it off, and in the movie, you can see me and him in that scene around the main character, as we were the only two with our helmets off. I will never forget that epic night of movie magic and being involved in the scene of a Hollywood movie.

The movie, *Never Back Down,* came out in theaters, and I will always remember the surreal feeling of sitting in the theater and seeing myself on the big screen. The football scene was the bomb and worth the long, drenched hours it took to create it.

After that movie, I decided to hire an agent because I heard that was the best way to get more experience, whether you were a beginner or seasoned. When you meet with an agent for the first time, they will most likely ask you to do a monologue of some sort to showcase your talent before even having the conversation about signing you. I did a scene from a Denzel Washington movie where he played a lawyer and gave a passionate closing argument to the jury. My nerves almost got the best of me, and I am sure she could tell, but after my audition, she asked me to wait in the lobby. The agent finally called me back in and said she saw enough raw talent and personality to sign me as a client and help me get started. I could not believe it! Driving home from the audition proved difficult since I was so high on cloud nine.

I came across a casting call for a horror film with four substories. I read the different roles and decided I wanted to audition for one of them. I had never auditioned for anything in my life and was not sure what I was doing. When I arrived, I told the people holding the auditions what role I wanted to read for, and they handed me lines to memorize and act out. I learned these were called "sides," so if nothing came of my efforts, at least I had learned a new term in the acting world. The room was packed with people. I began memorizing the sides and imagining what this character looked like and how he talked. Pretty soon, they called my name, and we went to a room where three guys sat at a table. They were friendly, which helped me feel at ease. I had to stand on the mark on the floor, and they asked me to "slate." This was another term I had never heard of, so I admitted I needed a quick reminder of what that meant. Slating is when you face the camera and say your full name, age, agent or agency name, and the part you are reading for. One of the guys read the other person in the scene, and I read for a character who was a vampire and came off as quite arrogant. They asked me to read it a few different ways, which I thought meant I was terrible. Acting lesson number three...if they keep asking you to try it different ways, it's a good thing and means they like what they see and want to see how directable you are. I believed I had blown the audition and began criticizing myself, even though it was my first time auditioning. A week passed without a word, but then I received a phone call. It was the crew I had auditioned for, and they wanted me to call them back. Could this be a good sign? I called back immediately, and the gentleman on the other end introduced himself as Steven Shea with Abysmal Entertainment. He was the director of the movie I auditioned for and told me he appreciated my auditioning for the vampire lead and thought I did well, but they went with somebody else for the part. Before I could be bummed, he proceeded to tell me they thought I would be perfect for one of the antagonist roles, Billy, and wanted to offer me the part. The word *YES* flew from my lips, and before I knew it, I had officially been offered a role after my first audition! I shared the exciting news with the friends I was hanging out with because I didn't want to keep this passion of mine a secret anymore.

The world was mine for the taking. *How could life get any better*, I thought. That was until I received a phone call from my agent letting me know a movie production was interested in me being a stand-in for the lead character. I had no clue what a stand-in was, but my agent explained that I wear the same clothes as the character, go through a scene hitting the same marks, and reenact the scene so the lighting folks can get the lighting set for when the actor comes on set. I thought the role would be a great way to learn even more about the business, so I said yes. The movie was being filmed on one of the soundstages on the Universal Studios's backlot, which provided an even better opportunity to see a major motion picture set that was built on a soundstage. It was all as I imagined it would be. The actor I stood in for was Garret Dillahunt. He is known for the movies *12 Years a Slave, Looper, The Last House on the Left, No Country for Old Men*, and the television shows *Deadwood, Terminator: Sarah Connor Chronicles*, and Fox's *Raising Hope*. He was a great guy, and I enjoyed being a stand-in because I learned so much about making a movie, from lighting to marking. A little boy starred in the movie, and I remember he kept throwing little candies at me from the break table. I sat with him and his grandmother for lunch, and in conversation, I asked if her grandson had done much acting and what his favorite project had been. She replied that his favorite by far was working with Will Smith. My eyes widened because Will Smith is one of my favorite actors. I asked when he worked with Will and she said he co-starred in a movie called *I Am Legend* that had just come out. It suddenly hit me that he was the little boy in the movie! His name was Charlie Tahan.

There I was, living out my dream of being an actor and hanging out in the soundstages of Universal Studios with movie stars. The impossible had become possible. Kidney failure was not on my radar or written into the business plan. But you know what they say about people who tell God their plans. At that time, I had not heard of the saying, but I was about to find out in a short time how wrong I was with my mindset towards my disease. If only I could have hit the control-print screen buttons of my life so I could paste it at any point during my life after I turned 23 years old.

At the end of the Disney internship in 2008, I landed a job in the National Basketball Association with the Orlando Magic right down the road. I grew up a big Orlando Magic fan, and I even had my room decorated in Magic colors, Magic pillows, and posters of my favorite players, Penny Hardaway and Shaquille O'Neil, decorated my wall. What a blessing to go from a dream job at my favorite place on earth – Disney World – to work for my favorite sports team growing up. I had the world at my fingertips. Little by little, my dreams were coming true, and I was so proud of myself for going after them and not holding myself back. I felt unstoppable, like a raging train, and I couldn't imagine life not continuing this way. I took advantage of opportunities that came my way, and I woke up loving life every day. Kidney disease was not even a worry or thought most days, but looking back, I suppose tucking my disease away meant it wouldn't overshadow my happiness. Deep down, I knew if I allowed my mind to focus on the negative of having a chronic disease, it would be hard for me to pull out of it, so I shut it off. Out of sight, out of mind!

I turned 23 in 2008 while working for the Orlando Magic. But then, my dream job suddenly became a nightmare portion of my life. I had to be on my feet constantly, especially on game days, and I began experiencing gout in my feet. My foot would swell up to the size of a football, and the pain hurt to the point that I could not put any weight on it or even put a blanket on it, Once again, that sizzling knife-stabbing torture sabotaged my foot.

I knew I couldn't continue that way and needed to move home to be closer to family. I remember walking into my boss's office and telling her we needed to talk. I shared with her that I had kidney disease, and that gout was a symptom that my disease was progressing. It was important for me to be around family and people close to me, and I needed to work with the doctors who were familiar with my situation. Thus, the most beautiful chapter of my life, or so I thought, ended just like that. I had never felt more freedom in my life before my time in Orlando, but at that moment, all I could think about was packing my things…and my anger towards God! Why did He take all of this away from me? My dream job! My opportunity to act! What did I do to make Him hate me so much? These were all questions asked by a young man who could not lean into his faith with an open mind of understanding.

Chapter 06

By Steve

IT SAID, SINGLE!

A fter I left the Orlando Magic, my gout continued getting worse. I had taken a job with the Tennessee Smokies, the AA affiliate of the Chicago Cubs, and had to be on my feet upwards of twelve hours a day on game days. I made it the full season, but I knew my progressing kidney disease meant the gout would continue to the point of unbearable again. Unless I had a master's degree, most jobs in the sports business were jobs that kept you on your feet, so I began searching for ways to make it possible to further my education. I applied to many schools, hoping to receive a graduate assistantship that would pay for my schooling. Many schools invited me to join their program, but they had no opportunities for my tuition to be paid for. Then I heard back from Middle Tennessee State University, and they not only invited me to join the master's program for sports business, but they also had a graduate assistantship I could take that would pay for my schooling. This was my only chance at getting my master's degree and finding a corporate job that would not have me on my feet so much, so I took it.

I moved to Murfreesboro, Tennessee, and began a new chapter of my life. My first semester went great, and I felt I had made the right decision. My job taught me a lot, and I excelled in the classroom with heightened confidence from my experience working in the real world before returning to school. Things were going well, and it was a sigh of relief thinking, for once, life was going exactly how it should…that was until it was not.

I got called into the athletic ticket office, and they informed me the money for the graduate assistantship had run out, so I would have to pay out-of-pocket to continue my education. This was a major blow that came after only one semester. I decided to go to Middle Tennessee State University mainly because of their Sport Management program, and my graduate assistantship would pay for it. Now what? I had to make a decision about my future and did not have much time to make it! Do I stay and finish but end up in deep debt, or do I try to find a full-time job and maybe come back to finish one day? The dilemma was difficult, but I had to figure it out. After much prayer and consideration, I decided to finish what I had started. God put it in my heart to stay. I could not definitively pinpoint what that reasoning was, but it embraced me like a warm blanket in the winter. It just felt right.

At the beginning of my second semester, I had a class with Ron, a fellow graduate assistant in the athletic department. I did not know him very well, but he seemed like a great guy. One day after class, he asked me if I could do him a favor and help him out of a bind. He needed someone to join him in the press box for the MTSU Lady Raiders softball game to help play music, to make sound effects, and to announce batters. It sounded like a blast, so I said I would help him. I had a doctor's appointment that day, but I knew I had plenty of time to make it to the field before the game started. I left the class excited about this opportunity.

At the appointment, I learned my kidney function had gotten worse, and I needed to see a nephrologist. Part of the risk of staying in school meant I did not have health insurance, and I had aged off of my parents' plan. Having kidney disease with constantly changing issues made me wonder if I made a huge mistake by staying in school without health insurance. Should I have factored that part in more in my decision-making? Hearing that my disease was progressing, and my kidney function was at 30%, had me a little worried. The doctor told me dialysis and a transplant were in my future, and I needed to begin thinking about that. When I left the doctor's office, I decided to go and find the nearest dialysis clinic and stop in to ask questions. I had heard nothing but horror stories of dialysis, and to me, the best defense against fear is knowledge. That is why I went in that day and asked questions, saw a dialysis machine, and took the time to learn about dialysis.

Surprisingly, I was told I could talk to the Patient Case Worker in her office, and she would answer all my questions. I spoke with her for about half an hour, and afterward, she showed me a dialysis machine and how it worked. While dialysis is not ideal, I was intrigued by the process of how it cleans blood and keeps people alive. I thanked the case worker for her time, took some information pamphlets, and headed to the softball field.

The Magical Meeting

On my way to the game, I was struck with a bit of emotion about what I had just seen: a few people connected to the dialysis machines, and they did not seem happy. I questioned if I made the right decision to have a glimpse into that life before I even knew if I would end up on dialysis. The patients looked uncomfortable and depressed, which is exactly how it made me feel. What will I do if dialysis treatments are where I am headed? I had equipped myself with knowledge and insight, which helped me deal with the stress of the unknown, but I also gave myself a potential look into my future. Perhaps I can avoid dialysis altogether and find an amazing kidney donor one day. The odds of finding a donor are slim, but it very well could happen for me. I pulled into the parking lot of the softball field and made my way to the press box. Ron greeted me, gave me the layout of how the game would go and what my job would be, and introduced me to everybody.

After introductions, I sat down and got to work. Ron had a knack for making me feel comfortable, which gave me the confidence to do what I needed to do. The guy announcing the play-by-play for the student radio station mentioned his girlfriend would be joining us in the press box. The moment I saw her for the first time was etched in my mind like a heart with the lover's initials carved into a tree truck. Her beauty mesmerized me. The overalls and plain white t-shirt that she wore fit her perfectly and were complemented by her shiny white tennis shoes. Her bright smile brought out little wrinkles beside her eyes, and I immediately fell in love. Those tiny lines suggested she smiled often. She had elegant brown hair that hung to her shoulders, and the heavenly glow surrounding her hair grew even brighter when the sun hit it just right. Oh, my! When her stunning dark eyes connected with mine, I was captivated and thought, *Who is this girl?* I had so many questions about her, and the most important one was, why was she with the other guy in the press box? As I watched them interact, it did not make sense to me, and I knew she should not be with him. An overwhelming feeling told me that the guy wasn't her destiny.

Ron noticed my attention had been taken away from the task at hand in the press box. My goo-goo eyes were so obvious that Ron finally told me to ask her out. I played clueless, of course, but when Ron told me that whenever I cracked a joke, she would look over and smile, my big grin gave away my innocence. I made it clear to him, however, that I do not pursue girls who are not single, and I also reminded him I had just gotten out of a relationship that drained me. I was 25 with no desire to jump back on the rollercoaster of emotions known as dating.

Despite my objections to asking her out on the spot that day, I often thought about this girl. After a few weeks of seeing my "dream girl" at the games, her boyfriend finally introduced me to her. She and I shook hands in the parking lot as I announced, "It is a pleasure to meet you, Heather." I had no idea that a casual handshake was the moment of a lifetime, an interaction that would change my life. These are moments I call "God winks." God knew 25 years before that magical point in time that it would happen, and I swear I felt Him smiling down as the cool breeze cut through the hot sun that afternoon. Heather radiated kindness, and just talking with her left pure joy in my heart. Even though I had no interest in dating anyone then, seeing her with this other guy made me somewhat jealous.

Even though thoughts of Heather danced in my mind, I found myself still thinking about my kidney failure and what I had seen at the dialysis center. I convinced myself that girls would run in the opposite direction when they learned I might need a transplant or dialysis in the future, so my disease became a point of contention within me. To persuade myself even further, I answered the question, "Why would Heather even consider being with a guy who had "unhealthy" written all over his future?" I'm sure she wouldn't. Looking back, I realize those thoughts were more of a defense mechanism than anything. Who was I kidding? I had feelings for Heather and found her to be wonderfully cute and sweet. Perhaps I liked her more than I wanted to admit to myself.

A couple of weeks later, as I drove back to Murfreesboro from Knoxville, I glanced at my Facebook while getting gas. I could not believe what I read. Heather's relationship status read *single*. Wow, was she single now? Should I ask her out? Probably not; that would be way too bold, and my nerves kept me from ever being so forward. How could I find out if her *single* status were true? I came up with what I call the most genius dumb idea of all time. I planned to pretend to want to double date with her and her boyfriend one evening. That would reveal the truth if she were indeed single or not. It was a master plan and exactly what I did. I sent her a message on Facebook:

"Hey, I meant to tell you it was a pleasure meeting you, but I was in a hurry after the game. If I can ever find a date, we could double one night with you two! I hope to see you around the third floor!"

My phone finally dinged – a response from Heather:

"Thanks, it was a pleasure meeting you too, Steven (smiley face). We could double date if you like, but I'd also have to find a date. Will and I broke up last night."

There it was! The confirmation I needed to hear. My slick scheme went off without a hitch. Now, I just needed to find a way to see her and get to know her better. Before I could figure that out, I saw her in the library one evening. Heather sat at the computer next to me. Instead of working on our schoolwork, we were absorbed in a chat full of laughter and intrigue. Our conversation moved along like a free-flowing river with comfort and ease. I could talk openly with Heather without judgment. This amazing woman made me smile, and she also loved my sense of humor. Over the next few months, we talked whenever we saw each other in the library, which was often since she studied there and worked on the third floor. One day, everything came to a head, and our trajectory changed.

I recall talking to Heather in the stacks of books at the library for quite a while. That conversation lasted for what seemed like hours and continued as we walked to our cars. I remember quite vividly that she asked me to hang out that evening, but it was my idea to go on a walk and to the movies. I returned to my apartment feeling like I had just won the lottery! The girl I had doted over in the press box, the adorable girl in overalls with a wonderful smile, wanted to date ME. Ron called it when he declared she and I would end up on a date. Reality kicked in, but so did my nerves, and even more so than usual.

First Date

We agreed to meet at the Greenway, an angelic area of Murfreesboro, and go for a walk. My eyes widened, and my heart began to race as I noticed her car pull into the parking lot. She looked stunning! I never struggled with what to say during our long talks in the library, but this was an actual date, and my words seemed to have gone astray.

As Heather and I walked, we decided to make it fun by playing a game, which helped my nerves. We played "Factoids," where we took turns saying something about ourselves, hence the name "Factoids." We could say whatever came to mind, which made it the perfect way to learn about one another. We chatted about everything from our favorite pizza toppings to music and interesting facts most people did not know about one another. We had a blast playing this game and never experienced any awkward first-date pauses or quiet moments. The evidence proved we had a deep connection. After the walk, we went to a movie and saw *Iron Man 2*. I don't remember much about the movie itself because my mind wandered the entire time, contemplating the best approach to put my arm around her or hold her hand. Confidence has never been a friend of mine, so I struggled big time when it came to dating and making the first moves. After the movie, we talked a bit more in the parking lot and then called it a night. We did not kiss on our first date, which may have been because she had just gotten out of a relationship and wanted to move slowly. I was ok with that since I was nervous and didn't want to scare her off.

The Dance Date

I have never considered myself a true romantic. At least not in the sense of a gondolier-guiding-my-special-lady-through-Venice kind of romantic. I always had to make do with what I had available to me, and at the time, as a graduate student, that usually meant free walks and dancing in the headlights of my car. It also meant using bathroom smell-good objects from the local dollar store to add a rich and distinguishable smell of over-the-top lavender and vanilla in my living room to set the mood (and to cover up any uninviting odors) for any lucky lady.

On this particular night, I moved my futon out of the way, placed the usual smell-good gadgets around the living area, and lit a few tiny floating candles. I invited this most remarkable girl to my apartment and intended to have our first slow dance in my living room. I hoped this would win her over despite the aroma and lack of cleanliness of a single guy living by himself. She arrived and sat on the futon while I anxiously got my phone ready to play a song for our dance. The first song that came to mind was "Everything" by Michael Bublé. It was a fantastic idea, but I did not have a decent internet connection since it was 2010, and the internet on phones had not taken off yet. Regardless, I found my way to YouTube and the special song. I walked over to Heather and asked if she would please do me the honor of a dance. As we stood there ready to dance, I reached over and hit play on my phone, and the song began. Oh! It had worked out perfectly, and there we were, wrapped in one another's arms, holding each other as close as possible. No sooner did we find ourselves melting into this moment when the song abruptly stopped.

I apologized and realized the song was buffering due to the spotty internet connection.

This continued for the next ten minutes, and as the song continued to stop, we also froze exactly where we were in our dance until the music began again. I could not believe I had found the most incredible girl I had ever met. It took a four-minute song just over ten minutes to play, and we couldn't help but find the humor in it being the exact opposite of the romantic effect I intended. Instead of an epic fail, that *stop-and-go* dance instead turned into the most romantic moment for us both. Right then, I knew as long as we had one another and this song in our hearts, we could turn any situation into something momentous and heart-grabbing.

One evening, at the beginning of our relationship, Heather and I had a talk I vividly remember that revealed an even more wonderful side of her. We dared to venture into the conversation of money, or the lack thereof, in our lives. Heather told me flat out that she did not care for or require a man to pay for every meal, nor did it need to be a nice sit-down meal. We were both in school with limited money, and she recognized that. Fancy dinners and gifts were not her love language (whew!), so I acknowledged her wishes and let her know I respected them. I had no issue going to Burger King and splitting a burger and fries. The food didn't matter because just being together was the most important thing. This down-to-earth human possessed the heart of an angel. Heather wanted to eliminate any stress and worry for me about being unable to take her to nice places from the beginning. I will never forget that conversation.

Heather and I had not kissed yet, but that goal was high on my list. My gut churned with nerves as we stood beside my car, talking because all I could think of was planting my lips on hers. So, in a Sonic parking lot against my car, I found the perfect break in the conversation and took my shot. I gazed into her dashing brown eyes, slightly brushed the tiny smirk that drove me wild, and leaned in and kissed her. Looking back, I see this moment as a miraculous celebration in Heaven with fireworks banging as our guardian angels and God celebrated the moment of 24 years in the making. Two people whom God needed together had gone down such different paths, which finally led to that kiss.

Our bond tightened as we grew closer emotionally and spent many late nights chatting, laughing, and just connecting at the heart. I looked forward to having homework so I could go to the library's third floor and hopefully run into her. We hung out at Burger King on many of our dates and spilled our guts to each other about our dreams and aspirations. We joked how one day we would have jobs and afford to dine a little finer, and we fantasized about what life would look like after we both graduated and landed our dream jobs. Heather's beauty and warmness drew me in at first sight, but her intelligence is what I truly found the most attractive. The 4.0 grade point average in economics and mathematics that she maintained while also working multiple jobs as a full-time student, blew my mind. Plus, she still found time to participate in extracurricular activities and serve as President of the Economics Club. Heather's independence and perseverance became even more evident to me when I learned she had already paid off her first car while in college. I think Heather is every man's dream girl, and I often wondered how I could be the lucky guy dating her.

Heather filled my heart with love, bringing on feelings I had never felt before. I cared about her tremendously, but on a different level from past relationships. Dare I say a more mature level? Heather not only flipped a switch for me regarding being selfless and putting another's feelings first, but she also made me want to be a better person. She did not want a boyfriend who would be overprotective or cause a scene in public. This simple yet classy lady both desired and deserved a boyfriend to act like a respectful and polite man, a gentle protector, strong in his faith, who would listen to her needs instead of trying to solve her problems. She never came out and said these things to me, but I could read between the lines because I cared enough to notice her likes and dislikes.

When your heart opens up, and you fall in love with somebody, I believe there is an automatic transition in a man's thinking that goes from self-centered to selfless. You cannot pinpoint the exact moment it happened, but you do know that it happened as quietly overnight as when you were growing up as a child. That is why most people respond to the question, "When did you know you fell in love?" with a vague but true exclamation of "You just know." In the past, if you asked me how I knew I liked a girl, my answer would have been because she likes me. With Heather, I knew I liked her because she made me feel something special in my heart, made me want to be a better man, and made me see beauty in a completely different way. I saw both the beauty of the mind and soul.

Along with a memorable date at the beginning of a relationship, there is usually an extra special date that makes you realize what an incredible girl you have found, and that date will go down as "The Date" you tell your kids and grandkids about. Heather and I were blessed with that heartwarming and romantic date. It was December, and we had been dating for five months, so I wanted to take her on the most spectacular date we had ever been on. I knew large romantic gestures of fancy meals were not Heather's love language, but a beautiful soul like her deserved a fancy night out so I could show how I felt about her instead of just telling her.

Chapter 07

By Steve

A DATE SO SNOWY WHITE

W e both love Christmas and great Christmas music, so I figured tickets to see the Trans-Siberian Orchestra at the Bridgestone Arena in downtown Nashville would be a magical evening and the best date we had ever been on! I couldn't wait to walk through downtown Nashville all dressed up while holding hands with the most beautiful woman I had ever met. I told Heather about the concert a few days before so she had time to prepare and plan what she wanted to wear. This special night out on the town would allow Heather to dress up in a way that made her feel like the most gorgeous woman in the world.

A few days before our big night, I checked the weather forecast and saw they were calling for snow that evening. I love snow, but Tennessee does not see a lot of it, so I thought, wow, God could not paint a better portrait than to have snow as the backdrop to our special Christmas date.

I arrived to pick up Heather for our date, but I also had to pick my jaw up off the ground. Her beauty sparkled like the tinsel on a Christmas tree. She dazzled with perfection! On our drive to Nashville, I played a Christmas CD to help get us into the holiday spirit. Our excitement for our first real date was uncontainable.

The concert exceeded any expectations either of us had. The music, the performances, the lights, and the entire production mesmerized us. We held hands and sang along at the top of our lungs. Our smiles could not be wiped away as we witnessed the most enchanting performance. We were so caught up in the magic taking place inside the arena that we were unaware of the perfect picture God was painting outside.

As we left the arena, our eyes caught a glimpse through the massive windows running along the arena. The chatter of everyone's excitement about the perfect scene outside the arena overpowered the thumping of our hearts. It looked like our life had transformed into a snow globe during the concert. The snowflakes were as big as quarters and fell so swiftly that the snow accumulated before it could melt. Within a matter of minutes, the roads were covered, and the people outside turned into giddy school kids as if finding out their elementary school was closed for a snow day. Heather and I were just as giddy as the rest! She held my arm tightly as we navigated the snowy sidewalks. There were sounds of car horns, crunching snow beneath our feet, and steam that crept up from the grates, but yet the snowflakes falling seemed to quiet even the most boisterous scene of a large downtown.

The romance continued as we walked to the car hand in hand, still donning the biggest smiles ever. Once we got to the car, Heather took her finger and drew hearts and our initials on the car windshield. I remember looking over at her as her eyes glistened through the snow, and the moonlight revealed the brightness of her smile. There I stood, freezing my limbs off, but the warmth of realizing I was falling in love had me longing for that moment to last forever.

The slick roads made the drive home a bit treacherous, especially since we aren't used to getting much snow in Tennessee other than the Smokey Mountains. I drove slowly and with extreme caution to protect my precious cargo, and I did not want a wreck to ruin our perfect night. We were both hungry, so once we finally reached our exit, we stopped to eat at Cracker Barrel. Christmas decorations adorned the restaurant, and the fireplace was lit; it was the perfect romantic setting and the best way to top off a beautiful evening. We sat nestled at a table near the warmth of the fireplace, laughing and conversing about the concert as the beautiful snow fell to the ground outside. My dream date had become a reality, and nothing could ruin the most special night. My heart sat wide open right there, and I fell more in love. I knew I had found my forever soulmate.

After I dropped Heather off at her house, I slowly drove back to my apartment and just sat in the car as the snow accumulated on the windshield, soaking in all the happiness I felt. I did not want the night to end. The warmth I felt in my heart could have been enough heat for an entire building. As I took in the beauty of the snowfall all around me, there was one looming issue I could not seem to ignore. I was falling in love with this girl, but what if my health continued to decline and changed things between us? I did not want my disease ever to become her burden, nor did I want to put her through my kidney failure.

Chapter 08

By Heather

THE CONVERSATION

S teve and I had been dating for a few months, and one night, while he was out of town, we had a phone date. I decided to test the waters on the seriousness of our relationship, so I brought up the topic of marriage and shared a very personal story about myself. Up until that point, I had never told anyone about what had happened to me in December of 2003.

I told Steve I started praying for my future husband when I was young. As a teenager, I remember praying and being overcome with the feeling that my husband was dying. This made no sense to me and upset me. How could my future husband be dying? I had not even met him yet. Regardless, I began praying even more fervently.

"God, please allow me to take away my husband's pain! Let him live!"

Immediately, I felt an excruciating pain in my lower abdomen. The pain lasted quite a while, but I continued praying through the pain for my husband. Eventually, the pain eased and then disappeared. That event never left my thoughts, and I always wondered what had happened and often thought about my future husband's health.

At that point in our conversation, I paused. What in the world was Steve thinking? He must think I am crazy. I talk to God and feel things. I legitimately thought this might end our relationship, as I had gone too deep too soon, and none of what I said probably made any sense. I know it did not make much sense to me, but what came out of Steve's mouth next shocked me way more than I had imagined I had shocked him.

Steve: "Wait, where was this pain?"

Me: "It was in my lower abdomen."

Steve: "And when was this?"

Me: "It was right around Christmas 2003."

Why was he asking all these questions about the details of this story, I wondered.

A few moments of shocked silence, followed by:

Steve: "Have I ever mentioned to you that I have kidney disease?"

Me: "No, never. Tell me about it."

Steve: "I was not sure when I wanted to tell you about this, but after hearing what you just told me, it really touched me, so I feel now is a good time. I wanted to talk to you about my kidney disease. I was diagnosed with it back in October of 2003. The doctors had me get a biopsy to find out what exactly was wrong with my kidneys. During the procedure, they did not numb my lower back enough where they were going to insert the needle into my kidney. I remember the excruciating pain so vividly, and because it hurt so intensely, I had to beg them to stop. They took me back up to my room, and after a few moments, I began to feel an excruciating pain in my side and in my lower back where the needle had gone in. The nurse came running in, but it only lasted a few moments, so we did not think much of it and assumed it was pain from where the needle point went in. Fifteen minutes later, the pain came back with a vengeance. Both the nurse and the doctor who performed the procedure flew into my room. He took his hand and pushed down on different parts of my body and immediately said, "We've got to get you downstairs quickly." They rushed me downstairs to a CT machine, and after the scan, I began feeling very ill and nauseous. The doctor approached me and said, "We've got to get you into the operating room now. You have severe internal bleeding, and if we don't stop it, it could be fatal." I do not remember much after that, except I was extremely scared and confused because everything happened so quickly. The next thing I knew, I woke up hours later, and my doctor was standing there. I asked what happened, and he shared that during my biopsy, they accidentally nicked an artery, and it caused one of the most severe internal bleeds he had ever seen. He said when he went into my body to clot the bleeding, a miracle happened. As he approached the bleeding, it just stopped out of nowhere. It was the most severe bleed he had ever seen, and poof, it magically stopped on its own. The doctor then said, "Son, I do not know what you believe in, but somebody is looking out for you." That miraculous event had happened in my lower abdomen on December 19th, 2003."

All the years I spent wondering about that mysteriously painful episode finally made sense. God knew what He was doing so many years before we even knew of each other's existence.

ACT 2

By Heather & Steve

FIRST DAY OF SPRING

Steve

March 20, 2011

While working my part-time shift one day at the local YMCA so I could pay rent, my mind constantly wandered off to thoughts of Heather. I thought back to our dates at Burger King, how she laughed at my jokes, how her smile lit up the world, and how I had finally found the missing piece of my heart. She was the complete package and all I had ever hoped for in a girlfriend and partner in life. I began to tear up while standing at the front desk, and my co-worker asked me what was wrong. After talking to him, I suddenly proclaimed, "Today is the day! I am going to ask her to marry me!"

I recall rushing to the jeweler to purchase the ring I had already picked out because today would be the day. I felt it in my heart; I had prayed about it, and all my feelings pointed towards doing it on this day.

I asked Heather to meet me at the Greenway in Murfreesboro, Tennessee, where we had our first date. She looked stunning, as usual! I tried to act cool, but the butterflies were fluttering around my stomach with the sting of a bee. We began walking, and just like before, we played "Factoids" as we walked and held hands. I wondered if Heather could hear my heart beating out of my chest since I could hear it loud and clear as if I were equipped with a stethoscope.

We made our way to a smaller bridge that went over a creek, a perfect romantic spot. We stopped, and I began to profess my love for her. I could feel my hands beginning to tremble and my heart rate increase. With a lump in my throat, I declared to her my thoughts on marriage. She and I had talked about it before, so it was not a random conversation that caught her off guard. I told her marriage is something that should happen at the right time, with the right person, and between two people who are so head-over-heels in love that it must be God matching them together. She agreed with me and reiterated her thoughts on the timing of marriage. I stepped back from her and the bridge's railing as she spoke. When she turned around, there I was, down on one knee, looking up at her with tears in my eyes.

"I believe God has set this moment to be the right time," I said as I popped the question.

Heather began crying, and I was unsure if it was happy or sad tears, but when she screamed out, *YES!* I knew at that moment my dream girl had just said yes to spending the rest of her life with me. What Heather didn't notice was the pain in my face from putting out my back due to how quickly I went down on one knee. I kept a smile on my face as I asked her to marry me, and finally, she grabbed my hand and helped me up. As foreshadowing goes, this moment would encapsulate how our marriage would go from the beginning.

We asked a few people who were running the trail right past us if they would stop and take our photo so we could capture the moment. They had seen me down on one knee and were incredibly kind to us. Those strangers made the proposal even more special by cheering for us and congratulating us. They helped us recreate the picture of me down on my knee, and I cherish that favorite photo with all my heart. That day, God brought two people together, 25 years in the making. Moments like getting engaged are not coincidental, and it brings chills to my soul when I imagine how God knew I would be in that park at that time, the day I was born.

Heather and I began walking back to our car, hand in hand, on a feverish high over what had just happened. We both couldn't contain our tears of joy, and I felt a warmth in my heart that I had never experienced. The feeling of wholeness, safety, happiness, and as if God were hugging me encapsulated my body. I knew I had made the right decision, and I was already planning our future in my head. As we approached the car, we discussed where we should go to eat and celebrate. We chose Outback and received a free appetizer because it was the first day of spring. This would become an annual tradition that would continue for many years.

Heather

March 20, 2011

It was the first day of spring, 2011. Steve and I had plans for a date to walk on the same Greenway we visited on our first date. Being out in nature with the sun on my face, the wind in my hair, and all the smells and sounds of nature always puts me in a good mood. We had taken many walks and had many talks on the Greenway, but there was something about that day that felt different. Steve was taking me to one of our favorite spots for a special reason. I could feel it.

Spring was in the air, with change happening all around and between us. I arrived at the Greenway just a few minutes before Steve and waited for him in my car. When he pulled up beside me in the gravel parking lot, and I heard the crunching sound of rocks beneath his tires, a huge grin formed across my face when I looked over and saw the man I loved. He has a way of making me smile just by being in his presence.

We both got out of our cars, me out of my red Ford Focus, and Steve out of his grey Solara. I got out of my car as he turned off his ignition and got out of his vehicle. I immediately reached my arms up around his neck in an embrace, and he kissed and hugged me. Then we held hands as we embarked on the trail – an adventure that the two of us would never forget.

Steve seemed nervous, although still his usual loving self. He is naturally an anxious person, but not when it comes to us. We were each other's calm in the storm called life. His fidgeting tipped me off that something was up. For a split second, I thought he might be proposing today. Then, as quickly as the thought entered my mind, it vanished. I noticed something in his jeans pocket nearest me, which I thought may have been a ring box, but then I quickly dismissed that hypothesis because I remembered I had handed him my phone to put into his pocket since my outfit did not have any.

Not long into our walk, we reached a little wooden bridge over a small creek, and Steve stopped to face me. He began to talk about marriage and how timing is important. Then he got down on one knee and reached into the pocket that had been on the opposite side of me (not the one my phone was in), and he pulled out a ring box.

It was there on that little bridge, surrounded by nature blooming on the first day of spring, that Steve asked me to be his wife. I think I said yes, but I do remember bending down and kissing and hugging him as he got back on his feet and then kissing and hugging and laughing some more. He finally confirmed, "So, is that a yes?" I guess I may have left the poor guy hanging since I didn't come out and say it right away. A couple approached us on the bridge coming from where we were headed, and we blurted out, "We just got engaged!!" These kind strangers congratulated us and suggested we reenact it so they could take our photo.

Steve handed my phone over to the woman, and he got down on one knee again, and I said, "Yes, yes, yes!" With the biggest smile on my face. We hugged and kissed all over again, this time with our love and commitment to each other witnessed by people we just met. It felt as if I had married him at that moment. That "yes" meant forever to me, and I knew he felt the same.

The sweet couple congratulated us again as they handed my phone back and continued walking. The first day of spring is a day we celebrate every single year.

Chapter 10

By Steve

I DO

My stomach fluttered as I paced back and forth in our apartment, almost wearing out the rug beneath my feet. The next day wasn't just any other day; I was getting married to the love of my life. We had been waiting for this day for a year, and now the woman I had fallen head over heels for would be walking down the aisle to commit the rest of her life to me. We did not spend the night before the wedding together. She stayed with her bridesmaids, and I spent the evening with my best man, Tim Volk.

The forecast on our wedding day called for rain. I am a bit suspicious of superstitions, but rain, I guess, meant good luck. Tim and I got ready to head to the church. We took my car, a 2003 Nissan 350Z blue convertible. I loved that car! As we drove out of the apartment complex, we both heard a thump, thump, thump noise. Yep…flat tire! Fortunately, there was a Sears Auto Shop right up the road at the mall, so all decked out in our tuxedos, we dropped the car off and told the mechanic exactly why we were dressed that way. Knowing we needed to be at the church in a few hours, he put us at the top of the list. With some time to kill, we headed into the mall and scored ourselves some Chick-fil-A. This was momentous because Heather is allergic to peanuts, and they use peanut oil to fry their chicken. I knew this could be the last time I ate Chick-fil-A for a very long time.

We finally made it to the church and finished getting ready with my other groomsmen. We had the wedding at our church, Central Baptist Bearden, and our Pastor Bibb officiated. I looked out the window on the door, and I saw so many wonderful people there to celebrate our love. Two people in attendance who made our wedding weekend so incredibly special were John and JaDonna Puckett, Heather's Godparents. John walked Heather down the aisle, and we are forever grateful for them. They are two of God's most special people in our lives.

The ceremony was about to begin, and I walked out to the sanctuary and stood where I greeted Heather as she came down the aisle. As the song Canon in D by Pachelbel began, the tears flowed down my cheeks. Heather told me she had always dreamed of walking down the aisle to this song, and today, her dream was coming true.

Heather slowly walked into my line of sight as the back doors opened and the light peeked through the stained-glass windows. Oh, how I cried. God put us in the same room on that day at the softball game, and He knew the day was coming that I would be standing here at the altar watching as we became one. The smile on Heather's face, the flow of her wedding dress, the tilt of her head…oh, my! As I saw the tears form in her eyes, a wave of love burst through me like a broken dam. Her beauty radiated, and I couldn't believe she was making her way to me. The day had finally come for me to marry the woman of my dreams.

As Heather met me at the altar, I grabbed her hands tightly to ensure she would never run away. I nodded at my Best Man, who handed us tissues to wipe the tears from our eyes. I wanted to shout out, "Yes!" as loudly as I could at that moment. I couldn't wait any longer. Her veil cascaded off of her head, and it appeared as if two angel wings were behind her. Most fitting since she was, indeed, an angel on Earth and created by the hands of God.

We said our vows to each other and lit the Unity Candle, and the time came for us to say, "Yes." Through tears and a skip in my heartbeat, I spoke the most important "yes" of my life. Heather and

I had officially become one. Nothing is more beautiful than two people becoming one in God's house and promising to be faithful and unconditionally loving through sickness and health. What a powerful statement to carry a promise on. I knew I was chronically ill, but something told me that with her by my side, everything would turn out ok. God put it on my heart to trust Him and to love my wife more than I could imagine, and He would take care of the rest.

Chapter 11

By Heather

FLORIDA MAN...

Steve and I had committed to wait until we were married to have sex with each other. It was more my personal conviction, but he treated me and my decision with the utmost respect during the entirety of our dating relationship. Early on in our relationship, I let him know I was a virgin and planned to wait until marriage. Since I would only have sex with my husband, Steve would be my one and only. As our emotional connection grew, so did my physical attraction, and those urges were hard to hold back. I desperately wanted to seal our growing love for one another in an intimate physical sense. We dated for a year, and then we were engaged for a year. I almost caved numerous times during our engagement, but Steve remained respectful of my conviction even when my virtue waned. Due to financial circumstances, Steve and I moved into a small apartment together a few weeks before our wedding. At that point, I decided what was the point of waiting anymore. We had made our commitment to one another and were waiting for the ceremony. However, Steve found it more important than ever to hold fast to our commitment, which drove me crazy. During the weeks leading up to our wedding, he would not even lay with me in our apartment bedroom despite my requests. Steve slept on the futon in the living room every night. He would not allow any of my "temptress ways," as he would joke, and I teased him right back. I am honored

Steve did not stray from my plan even when I no longer cared. It proved his respect towards me, and that was such a turn-on.

As our wedding day grew closer, Steve said he wanted us to wait until we got down to Disney to consummate our marriage because, in his mind, that is when our honeymoon truly began. He figured we would both be really tired the night of our wedding (we were), and he wanted it to be special and not rushed. I was exasperated at this. An extra day seemed like an eternity. I was more than ready to begin this new phase in our relationship. We were both equally excited and nervous. Steve said that he wanted it to happen organically and did not want to put any additional pressure or expectations on the first time.

Despite feeling as if that night would never come, it finally did. Everything was perfect. We were at the "happiest place on earth" at the serene French Quarter Resort at Disney World in Orlando, Florida. The resort mimicked the feel of New Orleans with jazz music playing throughout, beignets (a fluffy fried pastry topped with powdered sugar that melts in your mouth) in the dining hall, and a boat that takes you to Downtown Disney with shopping and restaurants galore. After a wonderful evening at Downtown Disney and a boat ride back to our hotel, we snuggled in to watch a movie. We both felt it was time as the movie was nearing the end. We had been exhibiting affectionate behavior all evening, but as the closing scenes wrapped up, we became even more affectionate. The passion between us ignited, and just as Steve positioned himself, the news came on the television. Just as we were about to…the reporter announced:

"Florida man shoots girlfriend after mistaking her for a wild boar."

Talk about a mood killer! Ha, ha! We both tried our best to remain in the mood and pretend we did not just hear what we heard. Our attempts were in vain, though. How could anyone hear those words and not react? All I could think about was that dreadful headline – so unromantic! How in the world did that reporter say it so matter-of-factly? Steve kissed my neck, trying to continue, but as I giggled, he could not hold back any longer and blurted out laughing, "How fat, short, and ugly was she?!" then he rolled off of me. Laying side by side, we gazed at each other and erupted into fists of laughter. I even let out a snort-laugh, making the situation even funnier. This was not at all how I imagined our first attempt at marital lovemaking. Nonetheless, it was perfect and a great representation of our relationship – never taking anything too seriously, enjoying the journey more than the destination, and enjoying our time together no matter what we were doing. Whether that is making love or laughing at the most absurd "Florida man…" news story coming at the most inopportune time possible. I believe our ability to laugh and find humor and fun in any circumstance is what would get us through the hard days ahead in our marriage.

Chapter 12

By Heather & Steve

FOSTERING HOPE

Heather

My husband and I had a special dinner date on New Year's Eve. We always discussed the year's highlights and then our dreams for the year ahead. I looked forward to our recap conversations and to the coming year. During our conversation, Steve asked me very pointedly what my biggest dream for 2016 was. Tears filled my eyes in an instant as I tried sucking them back in, but I couldn't control it. Steve, somewhat concerned, asked, "What is it?" I sheepishly replied, "I want to be a mom." He reassured me it would happen, but I interjected, "I want to be a mom now." He chuckled and said that is not how it works. Unsure if I should reveal my secret thoughts, I finally responded, "I want to be a foster mom."

Steve leaned in as if asking me to tell him more. I shared with him that I had a friend growing up who had been adopted by his foster mom. Fostering had always been in my heart, but I was unsure how Steve would feel about it. It would be something we both needed to be one hundred percent on board with. To my surprise, Steve said we should look into it.

In January, Steve and I went to an informational meeting about fostering. Then, we continued attending weekly classes until we were licensed to foster. In June of 2016, we got a call for our first placement. They were two girls, sisters, and they came to live with us.

They were seven and nine years old. While we were walking to the park, hand in hand, one on each side of me, the oldest asked me, "Do you want children when you grow up?" My heart melted as I tried not to tear up. I said, "I have got them right here. I squeezed both of their hands, and we smiled at each other.

Things you often hear as a foster parent are, "Oh, I could never do that," and "I would not be able to give them back." During foster parent training, you are often told that the goal of foster care is reunification. This is a hard thing to grapple with when children are put in foster care, typically, for neglect and/or abuse. Steve and I went into fostering, with open minds and hearts, to love children for as long as they were entrusted to us. I am not going to go into detail about our foster children, why they were placed with us, or where they went after leaving our home to protect their privacy. Their stories are theirs alone to tell. I am grateful to have been a part of it. However big or small that part was, I am blessed for the continued contact I have with some of them. To the precious children that I do not know where they are now, I hope one day to see you again, and I pray wherever you are that you are safe and loved. Each of the children we had filled my heart with so much joy and taught me so much. I love them all so very much.

I was asked once if foster children are bad kids. The answer to that question is no. Foster children are kids that have had bad things happen to them. Foster children are some of the most empathetic, kind, compassionate, and thoughtful people I have ever met. Since many of them know what it is like to go without food, love, or safety, they are incredibly generous and loving. Sometimes, all they need is for someone to believe in them so they can reach their full potential. Children who experience neglect and trauma often develop behaviors for their survival. Fostering can be exceedingly difficult because of broken people and a faulty system. Children deserve a loving, safe home and a loving family. They are not to blame.

Steve and I participated in a foster parent training class once, which had a profound impact on me. It was a simulation of the foster care system. Initially, everyone was assigned a role in the foster care system: judge, caseworker, foster parent, foster child, or biological parent. I chose to be a biological parent. It was the role I least understood, and honestly, I judged. However, I wanted to better understand and empathize with the biological parents.

During the simulation, my "children" were taken from me and put with a foster family. The judge told me my first task was to have stable housing for myself and my children. I was given a few playing cards to build my "house." I was given a time limit to do this. I started to get stressed under the pressure as I looked up at the clock. I thought about how my "children" were with strangers. I did not know if they were safe, and I did not know if they were scared. I was trying to do something I had never done before with extraordinarily little direction and no assistance. The time was almost up, and I heard from behind me, "You can do it, Heather!" The voice was my children's foster parent. That encouragement was the push I needed to help me realize I could do it. In the end, I was the only biological parent who completed their task of building a house. I attribute that to the encouragement of the foster parent.

That simulation changed my mindset, and I decided then, if given the chance, I would do everything in my power to encourage my foster children's parents. I got that opportunity after a court hearing where I met the biological parents of our foster children for the first time. The mother looked completely defeated during the court hearing, bringing me back to the simulation. After the court hearing, I approached her. She was crying. I introduced myself and asked if I could hug her. I did not let go until she did, and I encouraged her momma heart as much as possible. I told her I could tell she loved her babies, and I believed she could do what she needed to do to be the best mom for them. I told her Steve and I were rooting for her. Several years later, she told Steve and me that we were the only people who had ever told her in her entire life that we believed in her. You see, children who are in foster care are often a part of generational neglect and trauma. Those parents were once children, too. Those children were not given the encouragement and instructions necessary to build their "house." Their parents also often were neglected and abused, and the cycle repeats. It takes patience, understanding, love, forgiveness, and relearning to break these cycles.

Steve

It was New Year's Eve, and we were at dinner talking about our future and what we would love to see from 2016. From the day I met Heather, being a mom was her single most important goal, outside of marrying the love of her life. Whenever I asked what she wanted to do when she got older, her answer was always the same: be a mom. I believe some women are born to be moms, and it is in their blood to give birth to, adopt, or foster children to share the extra love in their hearts. Heather was most definitely one of these women.

As for me, I knew I wanted to be a father, and I loved children and wanted to help them. Throughout my career, I have always used my job to find ways to help kids and create special opportunities for them. For example, when I worked for Disney, I would take a stack of tickets to the Braves Spring Training game and randomly pick families with small kids to give them to. I also volunteered for a charity called Give Kids the World, which was created and run by the Make-A-Wish Foundation for terminally ill kids to come and go to Disney World.

While volunteering at Give Kids the World, I discovered my true love for kids and for wanting to help them. Given I was a chronically ill person myself, watching these kids, whether terminal or not, smile, laugh, be kind, caring, and respectful, impacted my heart. I will never forget one evening when I was volunteering, I walked over to a child who seemed sad. I asked him what was wrong, and he said he wanted to meet Mickey Mouse, but he was sick and afraid he would not be able to. I explained to him that I worked for Mickey Mouse at Disney and knew him. The smile on his face was contagious as I proceeded to tell him that Mickey could not wait to meet him. Just that small interaction showed me how important it was to keep children smiling.

Moments like this one made me realize my heart had plenty of space for children, and one day, I would love to be a father. That is why I was open to the idea when Heather brought up fostering children. During that dinner, we decided we would begin our search and learn what we needed to do to train to be foster parents.

Chapter 13

By Steve

IT WAS 750...

W e began our married life together and bonded by some fairly traumatizing events in our past. Although significantly different, the trauma scars left were used as a bond between us. There is a saying that misery loves company, but in our relationship, it seemed as if our misery needed the other's company. I do not mean in the essence of wanting to be miserable together, but how it always seemed the holes left in her soul were the perfect matches of where I was whole in my soul to replace the missing piece and vice versa. Looking back, it was obvious that a freshly cut puzzle did not fit together as eloquently as she and I did. God had His hands on our lives and there are times when the work He does is so unbelievably perfect that you have no choice but to believe you have no control over your own life at times.

One thing Heather and I were always told during our first years of marriage was how you could tell how much we loved each other. We had always been, and always will be, the best of friends who loved one another more than you could imagine before we got married. Heather and I bonded so much over common trauma, and we both longed to love and be loved. Heather's genuine and caring demeanor is like no other, and almost to a fault, since that kindness put a target on her back for manipulators, mean people, and your everyday snake in the grass. I saw this happen to her many times, and each time it broke my heart. I had more of a defensive wall up that was also to a fault at times, and I found myself getting angry and defensive towards people and situations that seemed to harm her. This is where being somewhat opposites played well into our relationship and balancing one another out.

As our first couple of years of marriage passed, my health began to take a turn for the worse. I will never forget the day when things headed down a path that would control so much of our sadness, anger, fear, worry, anxiety, and even depression for the next seven years. We had gone to a movie at the discount theater and then to dinner. We were so used to pinching pennies from our college days that we continued the practice into marriage. Heather's degree in Economics and Mathematics provided her with financial literacy.

As we finished dinner, I shared with Heather that I was having difficulty seeing. It had been going on for about a month at this point, but I chalked it up to aging and being married (Ha!). While driving home, I told Heather I seriously could not see well, and things were very blurry. She asked me if I felt I needed to go to the emergency room, and as a typical stubborn male would do, I said, of course not. We were almost home when I admitted to myself that my vision was getting exponentially worse, and I also began noticing my muscles were aching. Heather struck a deal with me. She said we would go to the emergency room, and if the front desk staff thought I needed to stay, then I would have to stay. If they did not think so, then she would admit she was incorrect, and we would go home.

Needless to say, I was quite naïve at that point in my marriage. I walked into that emergency room thinking I was about to win and turn around and leave. I am certain I did not make it past "My wife thinks I need to be here" before they told me to have a seat and wait for triage. I walked back up to the front desk and explained my sudden poor eyesight, and they asked if I would like to have my sugar checked. For somebody with kidney failure, diabetes was a common issue, so I agreed to it without really any expectation one way or the other because I did not have diabetes.

"Mr. Winfree, we are going to need you to sit down. Please let us know how you are feeling because you seem to have diabetes."

This unexpected statement stopped me in my tracks. I asked about my sugar numbers, and they were over 700, which is dangerously high. They took me back to a room right away, and the next thing I knew, I had so many different intravenous lines connected to me. This happened so fast that I couldn't comprehend it all. Heather didn't leave my side when I was in the emergency room, and she refused ever to leave me. She loved me so much and wanted to be there for me no matter how uncomfortable it was for her, and Heather never went down the "I told you so" road. After multiple tests, the doctor came in and shared with one hundred percent confidence that I had diabetes and would be insulin dependent. Within a matter of minutes, my world completely changed.

They admitted me for a bunch of days so they could get my sugar down, and also teach me how to live as a diabetic and how to give myself insulin. One of the stay's educational aspects was educating Heather in case of an emergency. This education session ended up being a time of learning that went far beyond my loving wife injecting insulin into my body. The nurse handed Heather the syringe and showed her how to fill it with the appropriate amount of insulin. To my amazement, Heather took the syringe in her hand, wiped down the area on my stomach to inject the insulin, and then bam. In the blink of an eye, she jabbed me and pulled the needle out. I was quite impressed with how quickly she did it until I heard the nurse say, "Heather, sweetheart, you have to inject the insulin into your husband; you cannot just stab him." My eyes became wide with fear for a moment, as it felt like I had just experienced a scene in a Lifetime movie firsthand. Heather seemed much too eager to stab me, and the lack of concern on her face told me she had some things on her chest that needed to be released. Heather's sheepish apology to me became interrupted by her laughter and promise that she did not mean to come across so enthusiastic in her jabbing motion with the syringe.

Laughter has helped me cope throughout my journey, and a sense of humor goes a long way in maintaining some sanity. As I said earlier, I performed standup comedy a few times before my health crashed and my anxiety and depression took over. Having a sense of humor has been my saving grace during my hospital stays. The nurses laughed sometimes with me, and I could tell they appreciated it and also that I was not a difficult patient to work with.

Chapter 14

By Steve

IMPRISONED IN MY OWN BODY

*"I Have Been Down the Road of Hell, a Mirror of Reflection
Is Only a Shell, It's the Invisible That Makes Me Unwell,
so I Ask God, 'Have I Not Paid My Bail?'"*

– Steve

This part of my life is extremely difficult to talk about, and that is my battle with depression through all of this. I was already fighting issues of anxiety and depression before I met Heather, and I began seeing a counselor when I was in graduate school at MTSU in Murfreesboro, Tennessee. Talking with somebody became an anxiety-reducer and truly made me feel better at times. Vulnerability is not easy for most people, but I decided to allow myself to be vulnerable because being able to help just one other patient battling depression would make it all worth it.

My anxiety and depression took off when I experienced constant pain with my gout attacks. That dreaded and debilitating pain made me nervous that I would not be able to do my job, or worse, getting let go because I was seen as a liability. Unfortunately, that did ring true once my disease began to progress. I had never felt so disgusted, violated, and ashamed in my life than when I was discriminated against for something that was not my fault. I found myself filled with anger, which only added to a fire already full of anxiety and depression. My state of mind during these times was anything but healthy.

Depression and the words it spoke to me were quite credulous and debilitating. Every single day, especially days of dialysis, I felt worthless the entire day and was not quite sure why God still had me walking around. Dialysis came out of nowhere for me, like most kidney patients at that point, and ultimately threw my life into disarray.

My life had become exceedingly difficult for me; I was dealing with constant pain and always feeling sick. I was 31 and almost ready to give up. I had zero quality of life, and my depression had taken hold of me like a ventriloquist. My body was just a shell of the person I used to be – a stranger in Heather's eyes. I met with Dr. Nesbit and shared how miserable things were, so he told me to go to the emergency room, and we would go from there. Little did I know while packing my emergency room bag that my life would take a drastic turn.

Once I settled in a room in the emergency room, Dr. Nesbit came to see me and let me know they would be preparing me to start dialysis to try and get rid of the excess uric acid building up in my body. Just like that, Heather and I realized our family plans were diverted without warning. I would probably have to stop working full-time, making Heather the main breadwinner. Plus, we had just become foster parents.

If you are not familiar with the process of transitioning to dialysis, it is usually not a smooth process. You do not typically plan out dialysis and have the time to get your affairs in order regarding income, children, bills, or anything that will be severely compromised with the reduction of half the income. If patients speak up, I believe it will help prepare those awaiting dialysis on how to prepare best. Just as we advocate for ourselves in the hospital, we must hold ourselves to the same expectations when advocating for others who do not have the proper understanding.

While in the emergency room, I was told they would be preparing me for dialysis once they got me upstairs to a more comfortable room. The nurse explained they would create an access point in an artery in my groin area. This made me incredibly nervous and worried. When I was settled in my hospital room, they numbed my inner thigh, took a scalpel, and created the access for a central venous catheter (CVC). This plastic tube allowed immediate access to blood flow before or while awaiting a fistula to mature in your arm.

The time had come to roll me down to the dialysis floor, and fear was flowing through my veins alongside the blood because, as a kidney patient, you hear nothing but nightmare stories about dialysis. I knew my world had just stopped, and as far as I knew, it was over with for the time being. I remember Dr. Nesbit being there with me to explain how everything worked, and I'm sure to try and make me feel better. We had our picture taken together right before they turned the machine on because I had decided to try to document as much as possible about my experience.

For a chronic kidney disease patient, dialysis is something every patient wants to avoid. It is a nasty, time-consuming, and disheartening necessity that I came to accept since I needed it to continue to live. The idea of needing this machine to keep me going filled my mind with signs saying, "Depression and anxiety meet here." The immediate influx of mental health issues hit me and my self-worth like a wrecking ball. My mind moved a million miles an hour as I was rolled into the area blocked off by curtains for my first dialysis session.

When I become nervous or anxious, I tend to find reasons to laugh or make others laugh to lighten the mood. That typically manifests into telling a story to a nurse or very bluntly letting them know I am nervous. For this particular instance, I asked Dr. Nesbit to get a photo of the two of us to serve as my memory of my first time. He and I both cheesed noticeably big and then he explained what was about to happen and reassured me I would be quite alright.

After Dr. Nesbit left, the dialysis technician began prepping me for the session. She took out a bunch of tubing, injectors of saline, alcohol swabs, and anti-clotting medication to put into the dialysis tubing connected to my artery. My heart raced, which was evident during the blood pressure checks you do before you start dialysis, and my anxiety soared through the roof during my entire first session. All I could think about was how Heather and I would afford to live with the loss of my job. The nurse and technician did a wonderful job explaining everything to me, which helped calm my nerves. They explained how the blood comes out of my body through one tube, goes into the machine that acts as my kidney and cleans the blood, and then the blood is sent back into my body through another tube.

Dialysis patients have two tubes connected to their arteries for the egress and ingress of blood. When you look at what a dialysis machine does, it is mind-blowing. It took a genius to invent such a life-saving machine, but my anger at the machine then did not let me think of it in that manner. All I could digest was the idea of feeling worthless for my family. We had two foster children, and how would they get the proper love, attention, and dedication needed from a guy who was spending so much time every week in a chair hooked up to a machine and not providing for the family? These thoughts snowballed my mental health issues.

How could Heather manage to work full time as the lone income earner while taking care of me and the kids? What were we going to tell the agency? Would this be cause for them to remove the girls from our care? These thoughts continued like a marathon in my mind, creating a monster of anxiety for me. I could not sit still, which during dialysis is a bad thing as it causes an alarm to go off constantly. This alarm alerts the nurse to come to check on you and then restart the machine to make sure the tubing is fine. It always ended with a reminder to sit as still as possible to avoid interruptions. My lack of control also meant the more the alarm went off, the longer the session would take to complete. In my defense, it is quite the task to sit completely still for three hours whether you are having dialysis or otherwise.

When you have a graft, or a catheter in your chest, you won't need to have two needles stuck in your arm for the blood flow. If you are afraid of needles, there is that option to avoid getting stuck, however, there are pros and cons to every single situation with dialysis. While you will not get stuck with the catheter, you do carry a much higher risk of potential septic shock due to an infected catheter that leads directly to your heart. It is a very scary situation if your catheter gets infected, and a fever can happen within minutes of feeling fine. Trust me, I know firsthand.

Chapter 15

By Steve

THE MOST DREARY DRIVE

I will never forget the morning of my first in-center session at the dialysis center in town. I was already familiar with the process itself from my emergency dialysis session when I first learned I was diabetic, but now it would be my new normal. This was it, the dreaded drive to dialysis. The weather seemed a perfect reflection of how I was feeling as the clouds loomed so low to the ground as if to pat me on the back. The falling rain was misty, perfecting the dreariest backdrop. The dialysis center was located on the banks of the Tennessee River, so the low clouds had formed a fog-like visual hovering over the building where sadness was surely the inhabitant. I felt as if I was turning myself into the authorities after having a warrant out for my arrest,

The drive was quiet, while my thoughts were a battle of control between anxiety and nervousness. I was on my way to turning myself in and serving my time for something that was not my fault. With my bag of necessities (phone charger, nose drops, phone, and a blanket), I parked and took the walk of shame up to the front entrance. I had never wanted to be more invisible as the automatic doors detected my presence and welcomed me into the all-white insides of the building. The tile on the floor was white, the walls were cinderblocks painted white, and the ceiling was an empty and soulless white canvas.

I walked up to the registration window to let them know I was there to turn myself in. The seating area was not noticeably big and most of the seats were taken by fellow inmates awaiting their turn, and family members waiting patiently for their family members to be released. A few wives were reading books and knitting, and others were looking off at the walls. There was a door with a large sign that read in all red lettering, "Patients and Staff Only!" The door was not only locked, but they had covered the window to block any onlookers from seeing what was truly going on back there.

As I sat there and awaited my name to be called, I had never wished for a door to stay closed more in my life than at that moment. Every time it made a clicking noise, followed by the door opening, my heart sank as I waited to hear what name they called. Each time it was a different name, my heart would slowly retreat into my chest. The waiting area seemed to welcome depression with its bare, cold walls. Why wouldn't they incorporate some color and hang encouraging posters that feed us positivity and hope? My grim thoughts were interrupted when I heard the door click open, and a nurse called, "Winfree." My heart leaped up into my throat; I began shaking from nerves, and feeling as if my voice was fleeting as I managed to say, "Here." I slowly stood up and began my walk to the back, where my sentence would be carried out.

The nurse accompanied me back into a rectangular room lined with dialysis machines, and the occupants sat in recliner chairs with televisions in the middle of the room. All I could hear were the sounds of beeps, alarms, the quiet murmuring of nurses to patients, and a lady answering phones in the very middle of the room. Glancing around, I could not help but see the sad and disheartened faces of some of the other patients. When I got to the center desk I had to sign in and then stand on a scale that is built into the ground. They do this to get a before and after dialysis weight to see how much fluid was taken off.

After I stepped off of the scale, I was walked to my station, where I would be spending the next three hours at its mercy. There was a gentleman to my right and to my left who were both quite my senior and appeared to be sleeping. These two would now be my neighbors for three hours a day, a few days a week. My station had what appeared to be a Ziplock bag with tubing, alcohol swabs, headphones, and a few other items for each session. Since I had the chest catheter, I would not be subject to the assault of two larger-than-normal needles that are used on fistulas. That was the silver lining, or so I thought. The nurse had me place my belongings on the side of the chair and stand while she took my blood pressure.

I could not help but feel all eyes were on me as the new guy was being processed for the first time. I can only imagine the thoughts flowing through the heads of the veteran dialysis patients as they saw me, the youngest there by far, getting placed into my chair. They said I could not move much once I was connected to the machine as it would set off an alarm. I realized quickly that a lot of the alarm sounds I was hearing were the sound of the warden being alerted to potential conspicuous movement. Once the machine was turned on, I began seeing blood streaming outwards through one of the tubes in my chest and, moments later, returning to my body. The marvelous machine kept people alive but also carried with it a bittersweet relationship. On the one hand, I needed him, yet on the other I resented him. I did not care for his watchful eye and monitoring of my every move as if I were a flight risk.

As I looked at the people across from me, I got a glimpse of what I looked like in my recliner. I had my feet propped up with my blanket encapsulating me like a protector in the snow, and I had my headphones in my ears as I tuned in to the television that was just for me. A nurse or technician would come over every so often just to check on everything. In a world where smiles were rare, the nurses and technicians were able to provide a bright spot as most were so kind and caring.

Crazy thoughts raced through my mind during my first three-hour session, ranging from self-pity to anger. I was only 31 and had spent my entire adult life being sick. Now, my life had come to a sudden stop, and everything I had dreamed of and worked so hard for disappeared in the snap of a finger. Needless to say, this was the beginning of a downward spiral of mental health that would soon consume me and spill into our family life.

At the end of my first session, I felt excitement and a bit of hope as it was time for me to leave. I had served my time and was escaping! I was on my way out of the door and was quickly reminded they would see me again in a few days. I no longer felt free. As the feeling of simply being let out for work release overcame me, I realized that the feeling of freedom was just that, a feeling. I would be reporting back to my cell in a few days to do it all over again.

Chapter 16

By Heather

PIECES OF MY HEART

S teve unexpectedly had to start dialysis soon after we began fostering. He lost his job because they were not willing to work around his dialysis schedule. Then, one month into his dialysis journey, he went into septic shock and almost died. I was juggling being a parent for the first time while going from a two-income to a one-income household and also dealing with my husband being extremely sick. The ongoing stress this situation brought on gave me the feeling of being trapped in an underground cave without any air. It also brought on feelings of inadequacy about the wife I needed to be, the foster mother I needed to be, and the employee I needed to be. I had waited my whole life to be a mother and now my dream world was falling to pieces. Steve and I were not in a position anymore to be able to adopt, so our foster daughters were moved to another pre-adoptive home.

My broken heart ached. The girls left us two days after Christmas. They had only been with us six months but that was more than enough time for me to fall in love with them. My feelings of failure whispered loudly in my ear. I did not know if I would ever see them again, but on January 20th, Steve took me to dinner for my birthday, and as we got out at the restaurant, a car pulled up, and out came the girls. They ran toward me with the biggest smiles and with arms wide open for hugs. Steve had spoken to their new foster mom (soon-to-be adoptive mother), about how heartbroken I had been since they left, and they arranged to surprise me.

Steve and I agreed to put our foster license on hold at this time while we figured out things with his health. We called our agency and asked them to please not call us because "we cannot say no." I think all they heard was the "we cannot say no" part because we received a call in February for a placement of a two-year-old boy and a newborn baby girl. I immediately reminded our caseworker that our license was on hold, and we were not accepting placements at this time. It broke my heart to say no, but I had to put Steve's health first. I called Steve and told him about the call. He immediately asked me about the children, and I told him I did not get any details since I did not think we were entertaining the idea of accepting another placement. I asked him if he was considering taking another placement, and he said he would call back and get additional information.

He called me back and said they had already found another placement, but if it fell through, they would call us. The other placement did fall through, and we got the call. Those precious babies were a blessing, and they were with us for seven months until they went to live with their biological grandparents two days before Steve's transplant. We have stayed in contact and are now their godparents. After Steve's transplant, we took in two sisters who were four and seven years old. They were our longest placement, and we had them for fourteen months. Their departure from our home left us heartbroken once again because there was no closure, so we decided to close our home, let our hearts heal, and focus on our marriage. I hope all of the children we fostered felt safe and loved in our home, and I pray wherever they are now that they are safe and loved. I think of them often, and every time I do I wish I could wrap them up in a big Mom hug. Each child took a piece of my heart with them.

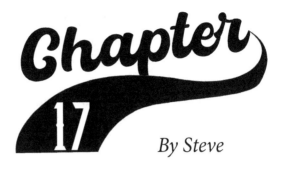

By Steve

HE MAY NOT MAKE IT THROUGH THE NIGHT...

In August of 2016, I sat in the parking lot of our local grocery store waiting for my prescription to be ready while munching on a McDonald's breakfast biscuit. My mind and my mood were not in a good place as my thoughts of my looming dialysis appointment later that day consumed me. I battled in my head, back and forth, hoping to justify skipping the treatment and instead spending the day doing other things I wanted to do. Of course, the little voice that always tried to send me down the best path was much louder, and like a good boy, I obeyed. I am willing to bet if you are on dialysis, or ever have been, you can relate to the self-confliction conversation I had in my head.

While nothing about dialysis was ideal for me, I knew I had to go if I ever wanted an opportunity to get a new kidney. Non-compliant actions with dialysis can halt all hope of getting a kidney transplant if you are waiting on the list. You must prove you are responsible enough to take care of yourself and the new kidney, and it needs to be this way since supply and demand are so far off. In fact, the amount of people in the United States in need of a lifesaving kidney transplant could fill every seat in a professional football stadium. I would hear other patients talking about their refusal to obey the rules set forth by their transplant center to receive a kidney, and all I could think was, "Why?" I guess certain vices, such as smoking and drinking, are more pleasurable than freedom from the dialysis chair that you are certain to be tied to for the rest of your life. To each their own, I suppose, but in my mind, I could not stand the thought of being married to that confining chair for the rest of my earthly existence.

As I drove to the dialysis center, I calculated the math in my head of when I should be done because I had plans to meet with the case worker from the fostering organization that we used to foster through. Dialysis is mostly uneventful (thankfully), but I had a sense when I signed into my dialysis session that day this was about to change in a very unfortunate way. I finished my dialysis and noticed I felt a little chilly, and I even commented on it to the nurse. Heather picked me up, and my chilly sensation continued to increase. We stopped to get her something to eat and I began feeling a little odd. I shared with Heather that I felt off and had the chills.

When we got home, I told Heather I needed to lie down, and she would have to speak with the case manager from the fostering agency without me. At that time, we had Madison and Emma-Leigh, who were our first placement foster children. The girls were wonderful siblings, and we adored them.

After I got into bed, I went from feeling okay to full-blown chills, body aches, and dizziness, and my body was burning up. How could this be? I checked my temperature, and the thermometer read 101.5, and then ten minutes later, it read a shocking 105. My fever had skyrocketed in a matter of minutes. I began moaning and trying to call out to Heather. She didn't hear my feeble attempts, but the case manager stopped the conversation and told Heather she thought she could hear me calling for her. Heather excused herself and darted upstairs to the bedroom. She saw me soaked in sweat, so she took my temperature. Her face went flush when she read the jaw-dropping 105.2 temperature. My moans and mumbles made no sense to Heather, and she could see my condition needed medical attention. Heather told the case manager she was sorry to cut the meeting short but needed to get me to a hospital.

Heather got the girls ready and grabbed a little hospital bag for me, and off we went. On the way to the hospital, I tried to figure out what just happened and what could be wrong. I just knew in my gut that my chest catheter was infected. That had been a big fear in the back of my mind since starting dialysis, and I knew it could lead to septic shock. I began to worry, but I hid my panic since I didn't want to frighten the girls or add additional stress to Heather's already strained nerves.

We arrived at the emergency room, and Heather grabbed a wheelchair for me since I couldn't walk steady at this point. They checked my temperature at the registration window, which came back at 105. I sat there doubled over in the wheelchair, trying my hardest not to seem too sick in front of the kids. Our foster daughters were just nine and seven, but they were extremely bright and they could tell I was not feeling well.

They called my name promptly, so I didn't have to sit too long in misery. A nurse rolled me back to a room and began the quiz on my health history. Things began to blur, and doctors and nurses rushed in and out, taking my blood, and they gave me something to help with the pain. Oddly enough, the pain medicine did not work, which left me very much incapacitated and doubled over.

It became clear things were not good when they ran some blood tests and came back to tell me I was in septic shock, and there were signs infection was spreading into my organs. My fear had been sepsis, which is an infection of your blood. My blood pressure had dropped so far that they could not give me any medicine for pain because pain medications naturally lower your heart rate.

I heard a nurse outside my room talking to another nurse about the shift change, and she made a comment about the seriousness of my condition and that I was being sent to the ICU as soon as a bed opened up. Once I heard that, I began to realize how serious things were, and I became frightened and began fearing the worst. The pain I felt was no joke. I could not recall ever feeling that terrible.

A doctor had come in and removed my chest catheter and told me I needed to be operated on. They were going to clean out the infection and tunnel the area where the catheter entered my chest and down into my heart. Since we had the kids with us, Heather could not stay the night with me, and no one we knew could help watch them for the night. I know, looking back, that Heather not being at the hospital with me the entire time ate her up with anxiety and worry.

Since a bed was not available in the ICU, they put me in a temporary room and proceeded to check on me as if I were in the ICU. I had the worst headache of my life at this point, and every time I coughed, my head nearly exploded from the pressure, or so it felt. I didn't sleep a wink that night, and things continued to spiral downward. The phlebotomist came in to draw blood, which proved to be nearly impossible. I am more difficult to stick due to my deep and small veins, and being dehydrated from the fever made it even tougher. They had to poke me fifteen times until they found some blood. As a phlebotomist, you can only stick a patient twice before calling for assistance. It took seven different people attempting to draw blood from me, sticking me between my fingers, toes, wrist, and neck, causing immense pain. It finally took a team with an ultrasound machine to do a guided blood draw before finally getting what they needed.

When an ICU room opened up, I remember being rolled into the room with nurses and technicians running around like chickens with their heads cut off trying to get me set up the way I needed to be. This intense treatment and care reaffirmed my serious condition. My fear heightened even more, and all I could think about was how I wanted to be with my wife. Very late into the night and shortly after arriving in the ICU, they wheeled me to an operating waiting area until the doctors were ready to operate.

There I lay absolutely miserable and so thirsty from being dehydrated, but I could not drink anything before the operation. Instead, they gave me sponges on a stick that were soaked in lemon water, which were for patients who needed fluid but could not consume any due to an operation. I will never forget the bitter taste of that sponge. Memories from that awful hospital stay make me shiver every time they surface.

Once in the operating room, a doctor named Dr. Michael Buckley explained in detail everything he would be doing and reassured me that he and his team would take excellent care of me. That's all I remember until I woke up back in the ICU, still feeling terrible, but things had escalated. Every twenty minutes or so, I had diarrhea and threw up, so somebody had to come in and clean me off since I could not control my bowels and the vomiting due to the infection ravaging my body. I didn't want to live in so much pain, but I did not want to die. All I could think of was how I would give anything to be with my wife. I needed her so badly I had tears coming down my face. My nurse asked me what was wrong, and I told her I was afraid of dying and leaving my wife and our foster kids behind. She assured me that people can and do survive sepsis, so I needed to keep fighting. At this point, I fell asleep and slept most of the day. I had no clue who was in my room; an entire day or two was a complete blur.

I later learned from Heather what happened while I was in the ICU and how she probably saved my life. I was out cold and had no idea she was in the room and had climbed into the hospital bed with me. Hearing Heather tell me how she wanted to memorize every part of me, my face, my arms, my legs, and begin talking to me, touched my soul and broke my heart, knowing the pain she went through. She then shared how she pleaded with the Lord not to leave the hospital a widow, and she did the one thing that had always meant so much to both of us: singing our song to bring me back to life. Heather began singing our song into my ear, with tears pouring down her cheeks. She prayed for God to please help me wake up and begin to heal. All she wanted was for me to hear how much she loved me.

God heard Heather's prayers and spared my life. The next day, my vital signs showed improvement, and it appeared I had survived the worst of septic shock. I do not believe it was a coincidence that God healed me when Heather prayed for me, prayed over me, and showed the most selfless acts of love and devotion. I believe true love for your soulmate is an unshakeable power. True love, and to be so loved, is one of the greatest gifts God can give us. My gratitude to God for allowing me to rejoin my soulmate in this life journey is never-ending. Heather saved my life; she must be my guardian angel.

Chapter 18

By Heather

SAVED BY THE BELL

I begged and pleaded with him to stay with me. Wasn't I enough? How could he do this to me? All while my inner self questioned if I was the one being selfish. If he were in so much pain, how could I ask him to stay? I love him more than anything. I did not want him to hurt any longer, but I also could not imagine the hurt of his leaving me and my having to live the rest of my life without him.

Steve had been struggling, more so than ever since starting dialysis, with his mental health, anxiety, depression, and feelings of worthlessness. He grabbed one of the knives from the kitchen block and told me what he planned to do with it as I screamed in protest. He held the kitchen knife to his arm fistula (a surgical fusing of his vein and artery that was created to increase the blood flow to speed up the process of dialysis, where they put a thick needle in your arm to pull the blood from your body and then put it back in once it has been cleansed of toxins). He planned to sever the fistula, releasing all the blood from his body and freeing himself from the pain of living.

I had often laid my head on his dialysis arm up against his fistula. Sometimes, I cuddled up to him at night in bed, and it soothed me to sleep. Other times, I would wrap my arm around his and lean my head on his upper arm as I stood beside him in church while singing hymns. It sounded like a rushing river, a current of life. I would close my eyes with my head on his arm and imagine a beautiful scene – a free-flowing river lined with fragrant trees, smooth pebbles lining the water's edge, the sun setting and glowing in the reflection of the water. It soothed me. This was his lifeline, the vessel that connected to a machine twice weekly that kept him alive. This was not how he saw it, though. To Steve, the fistula acted like the shackles that chained him to the dialysis machine. It felt more like a life sentence than life support at times. I imagined that river rushing, but now it was not a symbol of life, as if he were Moses during the first plague where he lifted his staff, only his was a knife, and he turned the Nile River into blood. What previously symbolized life was transformed into a plague of death. The thought of a river of blood never terrified me in Sunday school, but it terrified me now as Steve stood before me so determined.

I tried to change his mind. Furiously, I pleaded with him and physically grappled with him when he did not want to listen. I tried to wrestle that knife out of his hand. I tried to show him his life was worth fighting for and worth living.

My efforts seemed futile as his 6'2" body towered over my 5'6" body. He held the knife far above where my hands could reach. Angry tears rolled down from his eyes, not at me but at his situation, and mixed with my tears of desperation as they fell on my face. We both screamed and pled with each other. "Please do not leave me!" "Please let me go!" Both desperately pleading, fearing what our futures might be if the other would not relent. As I clawed at him to release the weapon that he wielded at my best friend, we ended up on the kitchen floor, crying and grappling for the knife. He eventually relented and succumbed to my pleas, only because his desire to hurt himself was outweighed, only slightly, by his desire not to hurt me. As he collapsed into defeat, we both were startled. The doorbell rang. We stared wide-eyed at each other, red eyes and out of breath as we recalled our new refrigerator was scheduled to be delivered today. We got up off the kitchen floor. As I went to answer the door, he looked over his shoulder at me once before retreating to the bedroom.

I feared he would take this opportunity to go through his plan with whatever he could find in our bedroom or bathroom, but I could no longer fight with him. I was exhausted. How could the man I love also be the man I hate? This man wanted to murder my best friend. I felt so alone.

To my relief, he did not go through with it. However, that day profoundly impacted me, and I don't think I will ever shake it. I remember later that month, I was going to a Christian women's conference for foster moms. We had arranged for our foster children to stay with a foster family friend of ours for respite care. I went back and forth on whether or not I should go. I desperately needed the retreat, but Steve was still in and out of an emotional crisis. The anxiety of the thought of losing him was still so raw. It is as if when he wielded that knife, he cut me deeper than any topical wound could ever cut. He pierced straight to my soul. The life leaked out of me any time I thought of it. I felt as if, by thinking of killing himself that day, he had killed a part of me. The complete trust and safety I had felt with him had been altered, and I now lived with a man who wanted to take away from me what was most precious. I grappled with grief, anger, and fear of loss daily. Afraid to bring up if he was still contemplating violently leaving me, I mostly just lived in fear.

Ultimately, I decided I needed to take care of my mental, emotional, and spiritual well-being if I ever planned to be able to help Steve come out of the dark place he was in. He encouraged me to go and assured me that he would be okay. So, I went. Many tears were shed while on this retreat. I prayed, worshipped, wept, and slept, and by the end of the weekend, my soul felt refreshed.

On Sunday, when it had come time to pack up and return home, I called Steve to let him know I would be heading home soon. Voicemail. I thought he must still be sleeping. Later that morning, I texted him. No return. Several more times that morning, I sent him messages because, at first, I thought nothing of his lack of replies. I hoped he was getting rest too this weekend, but my calm soon turned to panic as it became later. By noon, when I got in my car to drive home, I had called and left numerous text messages, none of which he responded to. Our kitchen, the knife, and his fistula flashed through my memory in a horrific movie scene sequence. Suddenly, it became hard to breathe as I envisioned why he was not answering. I drove faster than I ever had in all my life.

Once I pulled into the driveway, I ran to the house without even taking the keys out of the car ignition. I shook the house doorknob furiously to find it was locked. I banged loudly, both fists on the door. No answer. Steve always unlocks the front door for me when I am on my way home; if it is dark outside, he will always turn on the front porch light for me. Panic morphed into hysterics at this point when my banging on the door resulted in no response. I ran back to the car to get the keys to unlock the door. My hands shaking, I struggled to unlock the door.

Once unlocked, I flung the door open and yelled for Steve. I ran to our bedroom. The first thing that caught my eye was a pill bottle on his nightstand. Then my eyes saw him lying in the bed. I ran in and flung myself onto the bed beside him. Screaming, crying. He moved and put his arm around me. I cried into his shirtless chest, "I thought you were gone." He said he had not been able to fall asleep until around 4 a.m. He could see I was upset, so he wrapped his arms around me like a big spoon. I laid my head on his fistula arm, my tears soaking the side of my face, hair, and his arm. I let the sound of his blood coursing through his veins soothe me back to reality. Hearing the sound of life still flowing through him slowly eased my panic.

That weekend was a turning point for the both of us in our journey toward healing. We decided to speak to a therapist, both separately and together, to work on crawling out of the dark hole we were buried in. Many exceedingly difficult conversations were had, both in and outside of therapy. It tore Steve up to know how his actions affected me, and he swore never to hurt me in that way again. We learned to communicate better and support one another. We were no longer afraid of having difficult conversations because we knew the thoughts that remained hidden could cause the most damage. Steve slowly started to love himself again and find joy and peace even through difficult circumstances. My heart began to heal seeing Steve learning to love himself; there is so very much to love.

If you are in crisis, call the U.S. National Suicide Prevention Lifeline, a free, 24-hour hotline, at 1-800-273-8255. If your issue is an emergency, call 911 or go to your nearest emergency room. Outside of the U.S., please call your nearest hospital for local resources. Please reach out for help! You are not alone.

By Steve

I JUST HEARD BACK FROM VANDERBILT...

I came home from the hospital in March of 2017, and I will never forget Heather finally releasing her emotions. Exhausted and mentally drained, my poor wife carried the world on her shoulders while I was in the hospital. This amazing woman is by far the strongest and most incredible human being I have ever met. She dealt with working full time and caring for our foster girls and me, but she never complained, asked for help, or gave up due to the mounting pressure.

After another hospital stay (thankfully not as scary as the prior stay), Heather told me she would go with me to my next doctor's appointment with Dr. Nesbit. She had enough of the ups and downs and uncertainties, and something needed to be done to improve my health. I was taken aback by this because I had no idea what she could do to help my situation. I wasn't sure how I felt about this, but my nerves were on edge because of the unknown outcome, and I feared being embarrassed or told there was nothing that could be done. Yet, Heather maintained her mindset that she was going with me to tell him what needed to be done. She had two kidneys so she planned on giving one to me.

I recall thinking to myself the process of donating a kidney is complex and much more than simply telling the doctor to come and get it and give it to my husband. Heather's matter-of-fact attitude about it all amazed me throughout this entire series of events. It seemed as if she already knew it would happen and she just needed a doctor to get the ball rolling.

Heather came back with me to the patient evaluation room, and we waited in silence for Dr. Nesbit. The awkward lack of conversation made my nerves more erratic, and I went back and forth in my mind with regret and relief about bringing Heather to the appointment. How would she handle the disappointment if she could not help her husband? Just then, we heard a quick knock on the door. Dr. Nesbit walked in with his usual friendly persona, and we began talking about my most recent hospital stay. That is when Heather interjected about why she had come along.

Heather shared with Dr. Nesbit how difficult it had been on the family with my quality of life practically being nil. My constant pain and sickness did not allow me to live the life a man my age should be living. I then explained to him how my depression took over most days, and I could barely pull myself out of bed because of it. Dr. Nesbit sympathized with us and opened the floor to our thoughts. Heather asked him, "Hypothetically, if Steve had somebody willing to give him their kidney now, would this be an option even if his numbers are slightly over the limit of when transplants usually occur?"

I tried swallowing the lump in my throat at this point as I feared the entire idea would be shut down, but to my surprise, Dr. Nesbit said he was all for pre-emptive transplants if possible, and the best place to do that would be Vanderbilt, where he had done his residency. He agreed with us and felt it was worth his reaching out to his former colleagues at Vanderbilt to see if they would take me on as a patient and help me get a new kidney. I could not believe what I had just heard! My doctor believed it was worth asking Vanderbilt

Medical to consider transplanting a new kidney into me as long as I had somebody ready and willing to donate!

Heather's proactive plan to alter my sub-par quality of life paid off. Had she not been so pushy about coming with me to the doctor, who knows if I would have gotten the chance at a kidney transplant? That doctor visit left us with hope once again, and Heather planned to reach out to Vanderbilt about getting on the organ donor list as soon as we got home. Her confidence in her plan had me believing it would happen without a second thought.

When we got home, Heather followed through on her plan and went to the Vanderbilt Transplant Center website to learn more about becoming an organ donor. She learned the process involved filling out an online questionnaire first, and based on the response to her answers, the second step would follow. They were basic questions that seemed benign and irrelevant, but they were the first filter for weeding out those who would not be able to donate. They asked questions about medications, blood pressure, surgeries, and blood type. Once she finished the questionnaire, the waiting game began to see Vanderbilt's response to her inquiry and their taking me on as a patient.

If there is one thing we have learned through my journey, it is the days are long, and the weeks are longer when awaiting such life-changing information. Time crawled at a pace of forty-eight hours per twenty-four, but before we knew it, Heather heard back. She had passed the first step and made it to the second step! Our excitement had us jumping for joy, and we told ourselves we would celebrate every little step and accomplishment in this journey. If you move past the questionnaire, the next step is taking serum samples, and they send you a few tubes to collect those samples. They mail you a box along with the lab orders, so you can take it anywhere you would like to have your blood drawn. Once you have your blood taken, the lab will send the results back to Vanderbilt for you.

Around a month later, we were preparing to celebrate my birthday (April 24th). We had two foster babies at this time, Travis and Kayleigh, who were two years old and three months old. Having these two as part of our family was such a blessing, and we got along with their family so well. We were blessed to be the ones to bring Kayleigh home from the hospital, so it was our first experience as parents of a newborn. Travis was a spunky and outgoing two-year-old who donned the cutest smile, and his laugh lit up the room. We had the opportunity to meet his mom and dad in court, and you could tell how much they loved their children. We also met their grandparents, Todd, and Christine. Todd had called us over to his car after we dropped the children off for a family visit, and we talked for twenty minutes. We clicked on so many levels and genuinely enjoyed getting to know him. Grandpa Todd was a sweet man with a heart of gold who only wanted what was best for his grandchildren. When the family supports you as the foster parents, it provides a more positive experience.

We were all getting ready to celebrate my birthday, and I had just gotten home from dialysis. I felt drained and just did not feel the best. Dialysis tends to make you feel extremely exhausted, with a loss of appetite and feeling as if you just took a shot of Nyquil. However, it was my birthday, so I wanted to push through it and celebrate with our little family. That is when I received a life-changing message.

My phone alerted me that I had a text message, and it was from Dr. Nesbit. Since he and I grew up together and went to the same high school, we had each other's phone numbers. The message read:

"I just heard back from Vanderbilt, and they are willing to bring you in as a patient and begin the process of a pre-emptive transplant!"

Wow, I had just received the greatest gift I could have asked for on my birthday! Heather was on the second step of becoming a registered donor through Vanderbilt, and now they wanted to bring me to Nashville to discuss putting me on their transplant list and begin the process of looking for a living donor. All those years ago, Heather told me she would one day save my life, and based on what was transpiring at the moment, it seemed it could all be coming to fruition.

We had set the date for my first visit to Vanderbilt for June 29th, 2017. I felt like Buddy the Elf anticipating Christmas Day! I would begin the process of being put on the list, and Heather would be completing the necessary steps to become a registered donor. She would also be joining me for all educational sessions as my caretaker, and in between, she would have her blood drawn, in addition to some medical tests and meetings of her own to become my lifesaver.

By Steve

3100 VANDERBILT TRANSPLANT CENTER, SOCIAL WORK, PATIENT EDUCATION

June 29th, 2017

We woke up early so we could get on the road and make sure we were on time for this special day. A day that could send me on a journey of major change to a possible new kidney. Heather's tests would potentially put her on the donor registry at Vanderbilt and also see if she was a match to save me. We were both excited and nervous because we had no idea what to expect. We didn't deviate from our routine when we set out on a road trip: stop at Heather's favorite bagel shop for a breakfast sandwich and then at McDonald's for a sausage biscuit for me. In my opinion, when McDonald's biscuits are fresh, they are the best biscuits in town. It is a rare treat for me that is usually only enjoyed on our way out of town.

We enjoyed our breakfast and were on our way to Nashville, Tennessee, which was about three hours away. We usually take turns driving, and the other stays up to talk and have fun. We discussed the potential of her being a match and what that would mean. We could not get over how cool it would be if she saved my life after everything we had been through up to this point. For the most part, it was always just Heather and I dealing with my numerous hospital stays, and she was always there in the chair right next to me. No matter how much I begged and pleaded with her, she refused to be anywhere but right next to me every night. She did not mind being woken up every few hours by the nurses and techs coming in to do my vitals and blood draws, just as long as she was with me. This day was special because it was two people who had been each other's rocks going to see if the ultimate sacrifice could be made to save one another. I say to save one another because to save my life would be to save Heather's, according to her.

e discussed what the operation could be like and if we would be able to see each other. We averted the topic of whether or not she was a match. Heather went through this journey knowing she was going to save my life. It was the most incredible, yet seemingly irrational, thought process she could have. The times I did try to explain to her the odds of her being a match were always met with a very sincere and genuine, "I do not care what the odds say." She made it clear she knew what she wanted to do and that God had it in His plans for her to do so.

I have had many people ask me how I could ask my wife to be my donor, and the answer is quite simple: I did not. Not once did I ask Heather to get tested. She remains steadfast in her story that when we were dating six years ago, she told me that I would need somebody to save my life one day, and she commented that she would do so whether we were still together or not. That is who Heather is. That incredibly selfless and beautiful sentiment has always stuck with me.

At first, I refused to allow Heather to test and potentially be my donor because I did not want her to undergo surgery to remove an organ, potentially harm herself, to save me. I can be just as stubborn as she can, and I told her I would not back down from this. But she maintained she would not either. The stalemate finally broke when she told me why I needed to allow her to do this for me. I will never forget that conversation. She said to me, "When you love somebody the way you love me, it is important to allow the other person to love you the most they can. My wanting to save you is not a selfless act because I gain a lot from it in that I get to stay married to my best friend for a long time. Also, if you were to deny me the opportunity to save you, would you want me going through the rest of my life feeling horrible guilt and angst, knowing I could have saved my best friend, but I did not, and now he is gone?"

When she had me thinking about her life without me, and the sadness and heartbreak, those thoughts pushed me over the edge. I would never want to make her feel that way, and I could never forgive myself if I were to leave her hurting so badly. After that conversation, I finally understood, and there was no way I was going to stand in the way of my wife wanting to love me unconditionally. Sometimes the best way to love your spouse is to let them love you in return.

We arrived in Nashville at our destination and stopped at the elevator to look at the directory. We found the words "Kidney Transplant Center" and realized our future was about to begin with the push of the up button on the elevator.

When we made it upstairs to the door that read:

"3100 Vanderbilt Transplant Center, Social Work, Patient Education"

Heather suggested we take a photo of me standing in front of it and pointing to the sign to mark the occasion. We had no idea of the importance of that photo at the time and how it would change our lives forever. We went and registered at the front desk and waited to be taken back to a conference room. There were a few other people there with us, and we spent the next hour or two in an educational session about transplants, what to expect, the operation itself, how donors are matched, and every aspect you could imagine about such a lifesaving operation. They were very transparent about the risks and did a great job making sure we left with a realistic understanding.

Once we were done with the education seminar, we went across the medical center campus to another building to the lab where we both had many tubes of blood drawn. This is where Heather began her portion of the visit. We each had a schedule printed out, similar to a class schedule, that told us exactly what our day would look like. During our breaks, we walked around campus and found some great food. We took many photos because we were so excited about the potential meaning of this trip.

We both had imaging tests done (X-rays and CT scans), but the majority of the visit was educational, so we could completely understand the process. I learned so many things regarding the transplant process, and one of the mandatory requests of potential kidney transplant recipients involved finances. We were told that due to the limited supply of available kidneys, they want to make sure each kidney goes to the best possible recipient. This means a recipient who can afford the antirejection medicines.

I learned I would need to have a certain amount of money in my savings account or have a plan showing how I would afford my meds before they could officially place me on the list. They shared that many patients raise money through GoFundMe and other fundraising. This somewhat irritated me at first. What does your savings account have to do with whether or not you deserve the chance at a second chance with your family? Why should somebody who is not able to work due to dialysis be considered less than somebody who is fortunate enough to still be able to work? They acknowledged my concerns but reiterated they have to make sure patients will take care of the new kidney so it will last as long as possible. Thinking a transplanted kidney could have been better used in another recipient is not something they want to talk about, but these are things a transplant clinic must consider since the wait list is so much larger than the actual number of available kidneys.

Another area to look at is the psychiatric perspective of it all. I had to meet with a psychologist and talk about my mental health. They asked how I had been dealing with dialysis and how I thought mental health could be linked to being on the transplant list. Again, these are all necessary steps to ensure that the most positive patient outcomes can occur with each kidney. Mental health also comes into play if you find out once you get to the hospital for the transplant that the donor, or the kidney, is now not available. This can take a toll on you mentally for obvious reasons. That disappointment could cause someone to come unhinged. You must prepare yourself mentally for any potential outcomes while on the transplant waiting list, and the medical team needed to know I understood all potential outcomes and that I knew how to prepare myself mentally.

I appreciated the thoroughness of the educational process and the psychology portion. Mental health is a big deal with kidney disease, and Vanderbilt considered it an important part of their process. For Heather's side of things, she spoke with a psychologist to discuss why she wanted to donate, and to make sure she was not being forced to do it. It is illegal to accept money for an organ in America, so they vetted her to ensure this was not her situation and that every decision she was making was of her own volition. During one of the meetings that I joined, the lady told Heather she could back out at any time, and the prospective recipient would never know it was because she changed her mind. They would come up with some kind of a medical reason to tell the recipient. The look on the lady's face when I told her I was the prospective recipient…priceless! I said I would know something was wrong if they told me all of a sudden that the kidney would not work out. That would make for an awkward ride home for sure.

The final meeting of the day was with my transplant nephrologist, Dr. Heidi Schaefer. The best words to describe Dr. Schaefer are *awesome, funny*, and *intelligent with a matching sense of humor*. We clicked immediately, and I was so thrilled she would be my doctor through this part of my journey. She made me feel comfortable when I talked to her. The silver lining is Dr. Nesbit mentored under her, and he is one of the most intelligent people I know. Dr. Schaefer shared details with me about the process and how a transplant works. She allowed me to do a lot of the talking by asking me questions, it impressed her that my wife was there getting tested to potentially donate to me. I could feel she was rooting for us, plus she made Heather and I feel so comfortable going through such a nerve-wracking process. Meeting Dr. Schaefer solidified my concerns that we made the right move coming to Vanderbilt.

As we drove home, we could not help but wonder what life could be like once I had a new kidney. It would allow us to finally do some traveling and see places we have always wanted to see. My always being in a hospital kept us from ever being able to afford to travel. Perhaps it would also allow us to finally start our family, which was Heather's dream. So many positive vibes danced in our heads as we drove home, and the thought of my wife being the person who saved my life seemed almost storybook and too good to be true. The odds were not in our favor; in fact, they told us those odds were 1:165,000 that Heather would be a match to donate to me. However, Heather's faith and positivity continued to persevere for the outcome she desired, and it never wavered. She truly felt God had set her on this path, and it was what she was supposed to do.

I knew the process of getting on the transplant list was a tad drawn out, but thoughts of *Am I deserving enough?* taunted me. Throughout my life, I had been made to feel that my disease was not as serious as it was. Since kidney disease is invisible to the naked eye, I dealt with inundated comments of, "But you look fine." Thoughts of self-doubt entangled with these types of remarks contributed to my ongoing battle with mental health. I nervously carried a lot of guilt with me about my invisible illness. Maybe those who questioned me were right? Maybe other people deserved more help than I did. These old thoughts crept back into my consciousness and began to interfere with my excitement over the entire process.

Would I be taking the spot of somebody who truly deserved it more? My alter-ego allowed the war in my head to ruin the confidence and hope I had found. I knew it was the unwelcome voice that was telling me I did not deserve to get a new kidney over somebody else. The devil whispering in my ear was winning, but I could not stop myself from being affected by it. I did not want to squash my hopes of receiving a new kidney, not to mention the mind games that doubt plays for a person on dialysis to think they are finally escaping the shackles of the chair. My desperation for good news and for something good to happen had me in misery. I worried about myself, but I also worried about what it would do to Heather if she found out she could not save me. The thought of her broken heart made my heart ache. I needed to pull it together and believe and have faith that God had our plan already laid out, and it would be what was best for me – for us. God was with us every step.

Chapter 21

By Heather

SHE THINKS HE IS A GREAT CATCH

On Thursday, June 29th, 2017, we went to Vanderbilt, and Steve and I both had our blood taken (around 12 vials each, I believe) to see if we were a match. Being a match to donate a kidney is not as simple as just having the same blood type. They perform various tests that not only include bloodwork, but also an X-ray, CT scan, EKG, and even a meeting with a psychologist. I went to Vanderbilt for two full days of medical tests. During this time, I met with several different departments and had the most extensive physical I have ever experienced. It was an exhausting two days. Not just from walking to different departments throughout the very large hospital, but also emotionally exhausting.

The first week of July 2017 was the most nerve-wracking week of my life, waiting for the blood test results. Normally, I am a very calm and level-headed person, but this week, I was an emotional disaster. Thoughts of getting that phone call saying, "You are a match!" consumed me, and fear and anxiety were knocking hard at my door. I had been so sure up until then that I would be a match, but now that the defining moment was approaching, I was scared.

At work, I found myself in a million-mile stare in the direction of my work computer, and all I could think about was when would that call come in. I did not want to make small talk with coworkers or even make eye contact with anyone, which was so unusual for me. I felt like all my energy was tied up in a bunch of jumbo bouncy balls in my stomach and that someone had spiked the balls down there in the pit of my gut. Like a ping pong ball, the bouncy balls were hitting every wall of my insides and making me sick. I pretended to work, but the person living inside of my shell wasn't productive that week. My cell phone made a home on my desk right beside my computer mouse, and even with the ringer volume on high, I must have checked my phone a million times just to make sure I had not missed that call. All day long I would peek at my phone and pace back and forth from my desk to the bathroom, cell phone in my hand, to try to expend some of the nervous energy. I had to remind myself to breathe. Finally, about mid-day Monday, I couldn't take the excruciating what-ifs and scenarios racing through my head. I made a conscious decision to surrender, and instead of focusing on, *What if I am not a match?* I decided to face my giant fear in the face and operate as if I already knew I *was* a match. The new conversation in my head said I was a match and would be donating a kidney to my husband. Anytime doubt crept back in, which was often, I would kick in my manifesting skills and repeat "I am a match."

This allowed my energy to switch to thinking, *Now what? How am I going to share the news with Steve?* I remembered back to our Vanderbilt trip when Steve jokingly said, "When you get the call, please don't text me if you are a match or not!" We both laughed because that type of news should be shared in person. Steve knows me all too well, and he knows I cannot hold in any news, let alone news of this magnitude. Surprises just are not my thing. Birthday presents, Christmas presents...I always blurt those out, "Want to know what I got you?" Card games with me are hysterical because I have no poker face. If my hand is good, my opponent will know it by the stupid Cheshire cat grin plastered on my face. I cannot lie. There is an innocence in my excitement that I have never been able to hide. Why would you want to hide something good, other than maybe so you could win at a card game?

While thinking about how I was going to tell Steve the amazing news that I was a match, I thought back on the last five years of our marriage. I thought about all of the hospital stays, and how tears poured as I lay beside him at the hospital that awful night I thought I was losing him. I would have switched places with him in a heartbeat, but at that time, I could do nothing. Then, I smiled as I thought about how we had made the best of the worst days, and even in those awful moments, how we laughed together and found ways to make unbearable circumstances fun together.

I remembered once, while Steve was hospitalized and suffering from a particularly bad bout of depression, asking him about his childhood and what he enjoyed doing as a kid. His face lit up as he said, "I collected baseball cards." We talked about the joys of finding a card of a player you idolized or getting a "special hit." From there it just became something we did together. Steve taught me about players and the different odds of getting certain special inserts and hits. We had a lot of fun collecting baseball cards!

Then a magical idea popped into my head! What if I made a custom baseball card of Steve and revealed on the back that I was his match? Then I laughed to myself because if I tried making a baseball card it would just look like a wallet-size photo with words on the back. I am far from a creative, crafty, or artsy person. If you have ever been on Pinterest, my idea of a craft would be one of those laughable "Pinterest fails" that they post next to the real thing with the sarcastic caption, "Nailed it." Since I knew I would fail at creating a baseball card of my own, I googled "custom baseball card" and found out that the card company, Topps, had a custom card-making tool on their website. Perfect! I started playing around with it and discovered you could customize a card with a team's name and the player's position, and hometown. I uploaded the most recent photo I had of Steve on my phone, which was a picture of him at Vanderbilt Transplant Center that previous Thursday pointing to the sign on the door that read "3100 Vanderbilt Transplant Center, Social Work, Patient Education." I put the name Steve Winfree as the player, Vanderbilt as the team's name, and Recipient as the position. I then wrote this on the back:

"Steve has had a lot on his plate. With his health issues, he has been striking out a lot. He was not sure how he was going to wind up. His wife, Heather, thinks he is a great catch, so she has decided to go to bat for him. Now, Steve will be a rookie recipient at Vanderbilt Transplant Center, where his wife, Heather, will be pitching a new kidney to him. They are sure to hit it out of the ballpark together!"

I smirked at my witty baseball puns. I figured they were sure to get an eye roll from Steve, which made me pleased with myself. This reveal encompassed our unique relationship – his love for baseball and my love for puns. I hit the order button and entered my card information for the $5.00 plus $6.74 shipping and handling. Then – more waiting.

Exactly one week to the day that we got tested the call finally came. I swear I answered my phone on the first ring, shot up out of my work chair, and walked to the stairwell. My donor coordinator very calmly asked, "Is now a good time to talk?" and I replied "Yeah." I had only been waiting for this call – impatiently, on pins and needles, about to jump out of my skin – for the last 10,080 minutes. She then stated what I had been telling myself since Monday afternoon,

"You are a match!"

I have no clue what she said after that. I sat down on the cold hard cement stairs and cried. They were tears of relief.

Once I had composed myself somewhat, I wiped the tears off my face and walked back to my cubicle. My coworker, Dave, could tell I had been crying and asked me if they called. I told him no and then sat back down at my desk and proceeded to pretend to work some more. A few minutes passed, and I received a text from Steve asking if I had heard from Vanderbilt yet. Then I lied…again. I told him yes, I had, but that they said the transplant committee was unable to meet yet, and we would not know anything until Monday. I could sense his disappointment. It felt sickening knowing the truth and not sharing it with him, but he **did** ask that I not tell him in a text, so I was just doing what he wanted. My internal justification made me feel better, but I immediately wanted to help him feel better. He had mentioned earlier that morning that he needed a haircut, so after texting him my fib, I suggested he go to Sports Clips and get the MVP because it might help de-stress him. If you aren't aware what an MVP at Sports Clips is, it is the more expensive haircut package at an already expensive hair salon. I am cheap, so the MVP haircut is a special birthday or Christmas treat. Knowing that fact was Steve's first "Cheshire grin" tip that I was probably hiding something from him.

Then it dawned on me that the baseball card I had ordered on Monday said it would take three to five business days before it would be ready to ship. I immediately emailed customer support and shared my story and dilemma. The kind customer service representative, Sabrina, said she would reach out to fulfillment and get back to me. She sent me the proof of the card through email, and said she would have the card overnighted to me. I thanked her so much and told her I felt like I was going to throw up from the excitement of it all.

Now I had to wait until I got off work. The day dragged on slower than a snail slithering through peanut butter. Finally, at exactly 5:00, I clocked out. Steve and I were meeting at our fostering agency for a scheduled ongoing training to be foster parents, so I met him there. Immediately as we entered the classroom our caseworker asked, "Have you heard anything from Vanderbilt yet?" Everyone we knew was eagerly awaiting the news. Ugh…I looked down and shrugged, "Unfortunately we won't know anything until next week."

When the class ended, our foster children were hungry, so we went to Burger King right down the road. I could not eat due to the nerves in my gut going ballistic. Steve helped me buckle the kids in my car, and I quickly crafted a game plan to allow me to go home before he did. I said, "Hey, it has been a stressful week. Why don't you pick up some baseball cards on the way home?" Steve didn't second-guess my suggestion (whew!). He told me the new Bowman product had just come out, and he wanted to open it. "Great!" I said, "Get two blasters and we can open them when the kids go to bed."

I didn't have much time, so as soon as I walked through the front door, I frantically searched for craft supplies. I found some glue and quickly attached the proof of the trophy baseball card to a piece of cardboard. Then I got the kids ready for bed and tucked them in. My nervous energy must have been contagious because they would not sleep. Steve walked through the front door and could see my frustration and asked what was wrong. I asked if he would try to get the kids to sleep since I was struggling with it. He said of course.

A few minutes passed, and he came down the hall. I eagerly asked if he was ready to open the cards. While he had been putting the kids to sleep, I secretly opened one of the packs and placed his custom card in the middle of the pack. I handed it to him, and he looked confused. "Why did you already open a pack?" he asked. Stumbling a bit on my words, I replied, "I was just too excited, I think that pack has a hit in it, and I think *you* should open it. Let's sit on the front porch, and I will film you opening the pack like you are one of those YouTube hobby card breakers, and you can go through and commentate about all of the players.

He agreed, and we moved to the front porch. My scheme was in full motion, and I was about to leap out of my skin. Steve took his assignment seriously and painstakingly went through each card slowly. He talked about each player, saying everything he knew about them, and discussing how the new product looked. All I could think was, *please hurry up.* I encouraged him to keep going because I felt there was a hit. Finally, he came to his custom card and let out a confused laugh. I urged him to flip the card over and read it, and Steve did as I said and read each line. I giggled at my baseball puns, and when he got to the part that read, "You are going to be a rookie recipient at Vanderbilt Transplant Center," he could not get the whole sentence out and tears rushed down his cheeks. I sobbed with him as I explained that I found out today, while I was at work, that we were a match.

"You could be getting a kidney by the end of this month," I said in a high crackling voice from all of the emotion.

Steve responded through tears, "That means you are going to be saving my life?"

I simply replied, "Yes!"

Then I shared with him how I had made the custom card before I even knew I was a match, and when I found out today that I was, I reached out to Topps, and they sent me the proof. I confessed I had sent him to Sports Clips because I felt guilty for lying to him.

I turned off the camera and then turned on *our song* "Everything." We held each other and cried on our front porch. To avoid getting wet from the storm that had just approached, we went inside and cried some more. Once we got past that emotional state, we discussed whether or not we should share the video. After all, so many people had been praying for us. We uploaded the video to YouTube and then went to bed because we were emotionally exhausted.

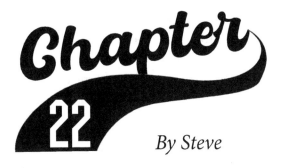

By Steve

NOW STEVE WILL BE A ROOKIE RECIPIENT...

July 6th, 2017

I was home thinking about how this could be the week I find out if I am getting a new kidney. I am an extremely impatient person at heart, so this part of the transplant journey was by far the most difficult. My patience was waning, so I texted Heather asking if she had heard from Vanderbilt. Her response, as you heard, was less than ideal.

Being the middle of summer, the outside air felt as sticky as honey, and the heat met your face with a slap. All the moisture in the air helped make the perfect recipe for thunderstorms later that evening, which made me smile. I am a huge weather nerd, and storms were always overly exciting to me. Just as I was about to succumb to the sleepiness and drained feelings of dialysis. I received another text from Heather.

"You should go out and get the MVP haircut and enjoy your day!"

How interesting was this? First of all, she never told me to get the MVP haircut unless it was Christmas, and secondly, she seemed quite happy for somebody who just told me that we would not know anything about the kidney until next week. I chalked it up to Heather just being her sweet self and realizing I was probably downtrodden from the lack of news.

As I made my way to the men's hair salon, I could not help but wonder if she had told a fib. I know her tone through texts, and rarely does she use as many exclamation points as she did. Those are reserved for special euphoric moments. During my haircut, I made the usual small chit-chat with the lady cutting my hair. But while she was washing my hair with the most wonderful, full-of-heat, and lightly-soaked towel across my face, I suddenly blurted out, "You know, I have this feeling my wife is taking me to Chili's tonight and telling me she is giving me a kidney over some chips and salsa."

I'm sure I caught her completely off-guard since she stopped what she was doing, paused, and somewhat anti-climatically said, "What did you say?" as she released a lengthy breath,

I explained my story and how Heather had tested to potentially donate her kidney to me. It turned out she had a close family member on dialysis as well. Once you start talking about dialysis and the challenges you face with it, you learn it is one of those things that affects more people than you realize. On one hand, it is relieving to find others who are traveling down this same path; however, on the other, it is sad to realize how many people are going through this journey quietly, and perhaps alone, as a battle within themselves. The saying "misery loves company" can apply to situations like these. Although most people view the saying as negative, I feel misery does need company sometimes. A chronically ill patient can benefit from talking with someone in a relatable circumstance.

I believe that is why I began telling my story once I began dialysis and felt comfortable with the conversation. I grappled for any glimpse of hope someone else might offer, or that I would find meaning and value within me. I was the rock climber whose harness had slipped and was praying for saving grace. Sharing my story allowed me to discover the meaning behind what I was going through.

I am a firm believer that if you take the worst thing about your day and find a way to allow it to enhance somebody else's day, then you have now answered the ever-looming question of,

Why me?

I thanked my stylist for the haircut and for lending her ear. She wished me luck and said to let her know if I am given a kidney over some chips and salsa. Heather told me to enjoy my day, so I decided to head home and relax before our foster parenting training class later that evening. It also dawned on me that we probably wouldn't be going to Chili's since we had the training class.

After my little snooze session, I met Heather and the kids at the foster agency for our training. While we were there, someone asked if she had heard whether she was a match or not, and she said no. There it was…she would not lie to them. I needed to get my expectations in check because being a match would truly be a miracle. The odds of matching were better than winning the lottery, and I still held onto hope. My heart told me to remain positive because anything is possible.

After leaving the agency, we met at Burger King nearby so Travis, our foster son, could play. As we were getting ready to leave, Heather surprised me once again by saying I should go buy some baseball cards at Walmart. Her unexpected sweetness confused me yet again, but I reminded myself to be realistic. Whether or not she had an ulterior motive for sending me on my way, I was thrilled to go get some new cards to go through, so I did not overthink it.

I made my way to Walmart and made my way to the baseball card section. I saw they had a new release for the year because it sticks out like a beautiful explosion of color and excitement yet to be seen during the year so far. The box had silver and purple tones, and the front featured Dansby Swanson, a player for the Atlanta Braves. That caught my attention in a flash because we are huge Braves fans in the Winfree household. I decided to grab that box along with some loose packs for us to peruse. My body tingled with anticipation of the pure joy I would feel when I got home and opened the dazzling assortment of cards to fulfill a collector's dream.

I walked into the house and placed the cards on the couch for Heather and me to open after the kids went to sleep. I went to say goodnight and tuck them in, and when I returned to the couch I could see one of the packs had been opened, but the cards weren't taken out. Did I purchase a pack that had already been rummaged through and that would be missing cards?

Heather came and sat with me and I shared my concern about the baseball cards. She said she was the one who had opened the pack, and she was excited to start looking through for treasures. Then she suggested we film my opening them because, at the time, I had wanted to start my own YouTube channel about baseball and baseball cards. Sure, why not, I thought and didn't think much of it. As I took the cards out of the pack, our foster baby, Kayleigh, started to get fussy, so Heather shut the camera off and made me promise to wait for her. When she returned, she said it would be more fun if we sat on the front porch swing to open the cards, so we headed out into the muggy evening where the humidity could be scooped up with a spoon. In the distance, we could see an emerging thunderstorm that was hiding our view of the setting sun. We sat and began to swing back and forth as the cicadas began chirping, which usually signaled the sun going down and a storm approaching in the summer.

Heather handed me the pack of baseball cards and began to film. My mind briefly pondered again why she had opened the pack, but I took the cards out and began going through them one at a time. I came across the best player in baseball, Mike Trout, as well as a rookie who had just been called up by the Yankees, Clint Frazier. I would make a comment or two on each player and then move on to the next one. The pack included the cards of Dylan Cease, Kenta Maeda, Anthony Alford, Noah Syndergaard, Carter Kieboom (whoever that is ha ha), and Brett Phillips. I chuckle about saying *"whoever that is"* with Carter Kieboom, because later on we would become buddies and raise money for the American Kidney Fund and catch a Major League Baseball game together. Heather had been telling me she thought she saw a special one towards the back, and I recall thinking, *How could she know that?*

After the Brett Phillips card, I chuckled in amusement as a baseball card of myself was staring back at me. I had no idea why or how it got into the pack at the time. Heather gleamed with excitement as I marveled at the fascinating card, and then she urged me to read the back. I complied and began reading:

"With Steve's health condition, he has been striking out a lot. [I gave her a "thanks a lot" look]*."*

Heather chuckled at her use of baseball puns as a subtle way to remind me life had been somewhat difficult up to that point. I continued:

"He was not sure how he was going to wind up. His wife Heather thinks he is a great catch, so she has decided to go to bat for him. Now, Steve will be a rookie recipient at Vanderbilt Transplant..."

What had I just read?? Did my wife seriously just tell me she was saving my life?! There were a thousand thoughts running through my head but I could only do one thing. My head dropped into my palms and the floodgates let loose.

Heather couldn't contain her emotions either, and through her tears, she muttered, "I found out earlier today that I'm a match, and you could be getting a kidney by the end of this month."

There we sat, both bawling uncontrollably in a moment that just changed both of our lives. My entire adult life, I had always been the sick guy, the person who was in constant pain, on dialysis, and who had given up all hope. In my eyes, I was not living but rather just surviving each day. The drops that fell from my eyes released years of emotions, ranging from joy, anger, sadness, pain, hopelessness, and depression. Never in my wildest dreams did I imagine I would hear the words, *I am a match,* coming from anybody, much less my wife. As the storm began to move in closer, we felt God embrace us in pure love...a feeling neither of us had ever felt before. That custom baseball card meant I had a second chance at life, and all because of God's grace, mercy, and love He displayed through my wife.

I finally got to the important question, "So, you are saving my life??"

"YES!"

Shock set in once again like I had never experienced before. My heart raced and the world around me stopped. I embraced the feeling of being safely surrounded by bubble wrap and nothing could harm me. My life was going to be mine again, and I wouldn't belong to the chair. The camera must have cut off, and the next thing I knew, Heather and I were entangled in the single longest embrace of my life. I never wanted to let her go.

God answered my prayer. Barely two days before that I was on my knees begging for Him to bring me home. I had wanted God to rid me of the aching beasts that had taken over my life. Perhaps the miracle came from my final plea, my release giving it all to God, or it is always darkest before the dawn. Whatever the reason, God knew I only needed two more days. He needed me to trust Him.

After our emotions calmed, I looked around and saw neighbors walking, I heard birds chirping and could hear children playing outside. Did they not know what had just happened? Were they not aware that God had just visited the neighborhood? The world had no idea what had just happened and that was part of the beauty of it all. This juncture between my wife, God, and me that had just transpired proved to be a testament to God's love. What was the natural next thing for Heather and me to do? Slow dance of course! I grabbed my phone and found our special song – the song we first danced to in my apartment all of those years ago while dating. The same beautiful lyrics my wife sang to me while I lay unconscious, slipping away from septic shock.

The music played, with thunder in the background, as the cicadas buzzed louder and the birds scrambled for cover from the impending storm. We locked eyes and never stopped, embracing one another so tightly as one. God joined our hearts together when we got married, and now, if all went according to plan, we truly would become one through flesh – through organ donation. God knew this dance would take place the day Heather and I were each born into this world. While the odds of Heather being a match were 1:165,000, God's plan proved to be a 100% guarantee. As we danced, all the pivotal moments of my life appeared in my head...the first time I saw her, the moment we shook hands and introduced ourselves, and the time we talked for hours in the stacks at the library where she worked...all of it!

That is what makes life exciting. God gives us the freedom of choice, and with that freedom comes the opportunity to take a wrong turn but also the ability to arrive exactly where we need to be at the right time. I had missed my turn a few times, but in this instance, every single turn, pothole-hit, near-miss wreck, or confusion on where I was headed, was spot on where I needed to be. At this particular moment, I was exactly where God needed me to be... dancing with my best friend, my soulmate, my wife, and my guardian angel here on Earth. Fourteen years earlier, I was a scared, nervous, and worried 18-year-old wondering what my future looked like. If I could go back to my 18-year-old self in the doctor's office when I learned of my disease, I would hug him and tell him, "Everything is going to be fine, just embrace the journey."

WATCH THE VIRAL VIDEO!

Scan the QR code:

https://youtu.be/Gn9IQ6qX08k?si=7wmCuaXqfVzN-YJj

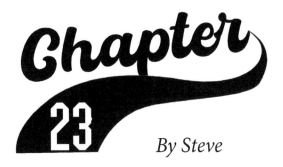

Chapter 23

By Steve

GOING VIRAL

A s we finished our dance, we went back inside to check on the kids who were fast asleep. They too, were none the wiser about what had just happened mere feet away. I could not help but wonder what journey God had in store for their lives as they slept so innocently. These little children were extremely special, and God blessed us with their presence in our lives.

Heather and I sat down in the living room with the biggest sense of relief, as if a five-ton truck had just been lifted off our chests. I knew I needed to share this most spectacular news of a second chance at life, so what better way than on social media? The thought of being saved from misery by MY WIFE coursed through my veins like nitro through the fuel tank of a street racer. I felt inspired; I felt excited. These two emotions had seemed non-existent in my life for quite some time. I wanted to shout it from the rooftops, so I did.

"I am getting a new kidney!!" I exclaimed on Twitter. Then Heather and I discussed how we were going to tell our loved ones, so we called my parents first. We did not want them to find out through social media or anybody else but us. After the call, we decided it would be best to let Heather share the beautiful news on her Facebook page. She didn't post a ton on social media, but she was connected to about 100 of her closest friends, family, and church family. The easiest way to get the video on her Facebook would be to upload it to YouTube and then post the link. Fifteen minutes later, she hit the post button, and we headed to bed. It took me a while to fall asleep due to my emotions running around like a two-year-old hopped up on sour straws.

We were woken up in the morning by the constant vibrating of my phone every few seconds. Heather noticed her phone going nuts too. We first thought it must be an amber alert trying to get our attention. I reached over to the bedside drawer and grabbed my phone to confirm my suspicion and at the top of my phone, I read "1000+" on the message bar. I shook my head and wiped my eyes in disbelief, then read it again "1000+" notifications. What on earth was going on? I looked over at Heather and asked if her phone was as crazy as mine was.

We took a quick glance and immediately noticed the notifications were coming from Facebook, missed calls, and emails. We assumed upon seeing the massive amounts of notifications that a lot of people must have liked and commented on our video. Having gone viral was not even a thought to us. It was amazing how many people liked our video and were saying sweet things. We did not think much of the missed calls since that happens every day from unsolicited callers.

We got up and showered to get the day started. Then we got a call from our local news station asking if they could interview us for the story that had transpired the night before. The reporter's name was Chynna Greene with Channel 8 News, Knoxville. We were flabbergasted that the news wanted to cover our story. I knew we had a crazy amount of notifications on our phones, so we figured that our friends on Facebook had shared the video and that it caught the eyes of the local news. Heather and I agreed to the interview and were instructed to meet at a park in Knoxville. It seemed so quick for our story to have reached local news stations overnight, but we were happy to talk about it on the news. Chynna had the sweetest demeanor, and we could feel her enthusiasm for our story. She shared that during their morning staff meeting, she was the only one who raised her hand to take our story and cover it. This made her happy because she knew how special the story was, and she knew there would be something incredible to follow. We were not completely sold on that, nor did we think people would care, but her excitement was contagious. The interview went great, Chynna made it fun, and then we took some pictures and headed off to lunch hoping at least one person would see our story and feel inspired about organ donation. Some people might find this hard to believe, but we had still not looked at our phone messages and notifications, but that was only because the morning had moved so fast.

Our stomachs grumbled with hunger pains as we arrived at Olive Garden to meet a friend. While enjoying their famous breadsticks, my phone rang, and I glanced down and saw, "New York City, New York." Why would I be getting a call from New York? I did not know anybody from there but I stepped away from the table and decided to answer it out of pure curiosity.

"Hello?"

"*Is this Steve Winfree?*"

"Yes, it is, may I ask who is calling?"

"*Hi, Steve, my name is Matt Stone, and I am the producer for* Good Morning America. *Do you have a moment to talk?*"

"Oh, wow! Hey, Matt. Yes, I can talk."

"*We absolutely love your story and would love to have you on* Good Morning America."

"Awesome…what story?"

"*Your moment on your front porch swing last night. Have you not been on the internet today??*"

"Wow! Did you see that? It just happened last night. No, we have not been on our phones much today, why?"

"*It is everywhere on the internet. Your video went viral overnight.*"

I went back to the table and Heather asked me who was on the phone. I asked her what we had planned for the rest of the day because *Good Morning America (GMA)* wants us to come on via Skype." The look on her face as her jaw almost hit the table was priceless! I told her the call shocked me just as much! She then asked if I meant "THE" *Good Morning America* show, to which I responded there is only one *Good Morning* for all of America, so it had to be. Plus, Matt Stone was such a television name. It had to be real. I explained that they wanted us to use Skype to do an interview which would air the next day, and he also told us to look at the internet. We both grabbed our phones, and the explosion of intense shock hit us as we glared in disbelief. Our little story of hope and love was everywhere – all over Facebook and Twitter. People we had never met were sharing our video and commenting. We each had hundreds of messages asking permission to use our video for their outlet and page.

We rushed home to prepare for the interview with *GMA*. Our nerves swirled like tumbleweeds as we tried to make sense of it all. How could something that just happened between us already be all over the country just hours later? The power of social media is the answer. We knew we needed to discuss what could potentially happen after our *Good Morning America* interview aired. We had already received substantial requests for interviews through Facebook. We had two options: ignore them all and just move forward with life, or embrace that God needed us to not only help others but to share our testimony about His love and miracles to the masses. We pondered and prayed about it. God wanted our help.

We set up the laptop on our kitchen table and waited with sweaty palms and rosy cheeks. All of a sudden it hit us, "What in the world happened in the past fifteen hours??" God happened!

We had an aha moment when our *Good Morning America* interview aired. Our foster son, Travis, who was two at the time, watched us as he stood in front of the television holding the baseball card from our video. He got so excited when he saw us on the television screen, and he began pointing at the screen with the card. Our hearts melted, and they always will each time we look at the picture we managed to capture.

Chapter 24

By Heather

GOING VIRAL, HEATHER'S TAKE

A fter telling Steve I was a match to donate a kidney to him, we held each other, danced to our song "Everything," then went back into the house and collapsed onto the couch in utter emotional exhaustion. Since I am a very private person, I was not sure if we would share the video or just keep it as a special moment for us to have and look back on ourselves. After talking about it, we decided to share it since we had so many people in our close circle praying for us who knew I was getting tested. I shared it on my Facebook page with my small group of close friends and family. The video was just over four minutes long, which was too long to upload directly to Facebook, so we had to create a YouTube account for me to upload the video and then post it.

It took us a bit to figure all of that out, so as soon as we posted the video we went straight to bed. We had lots of notifications in the morning. It was a Thursday, and I had the day off of work for the week of 4th of July. We had made plans to meet up with a friend of ours at Olive Garden for lunch, and I remember Steve getting up from our table at lunch and saying, "Huh, I am not sure who this is calling me, but I am going to take it. I will be right back." He came back, and with a stunned look on his face, he said, "That was *Good Morning America.*" I looked stunned back at him. I said, "Are you sure someone is not pranking you?" He said, "Yeah, I am sure, and they want to interview us today."

We were shocked that our story had reached producers in New York while we slept. Later that afternoon, we got on Skype to interview with *Good Morning America*. My nervousness soared, and I had a panic attack. I broke out in hives from the ball of nerves I was rolling in. Once our interview on *GMA* aired our phones did not stop buzzing from phone calls and messages. How did all of these people find us?

The intensity of it all felt incredibly overwhelming. I was working full time to support our family of Steve, our two foster children, and myself because Steve was sick, on dialysis, and fighting depression as he felt useless at his inability to contribute financially while he was so ill. Steve did not know it at the time, and he would not until I read this to him, but I cried so much during this time. His hospital stays during this time compared to a roller coaster ride…up and down all of the time. All of my vacation days were spent with him in the hospital, which was exactly where I wanted to be despite the difficulty. I had to request a leave from my work due to the amount of anxiety I was experiencing, and then when I did not have enough leave available, I had to leave Steve at the hospital and go to work. During the times we did not have foster children in our care, I would live at the hospital with him. That schedule meant I would sleep, shower, go to work for the day, then go back to the hospital. Exhaustion took over my life. I spent my commute to work crying every day. It physically hurt me to leave Steve alone. As soon as the work day ended, I could not get to my car fast enough to head straight back to the hospital. I felt so much guilt that I could not be in more than one place at once. All I wanted was to be with him, but I knew I had to work to provide for us. This completely drained me both emotionally and physically.

One day, I got a call from one of the nurses at Steve's dialysis clinic, letting me know he had been transported to the hospital. I immediately went to my supervisor to let them know I needed to leave early because Steve was not well, and had been hospitalized again. My supervisor offered no sympathy and very coldly responded, "Why do you have to leave? There is nothing you can do there. You are not a doctor!" I could not even respond to such an unempathetic comment, and with my head down I walked away and back to my desk to cool off. I desperately wanted to walk out but knew I could not afford to do that. All I needed was to leave an hour early. What was the big deal in the grand scheme of the business if one person out of hundreds of employees left an hour early? I am not a confrontational person at all, but my boss thrived on it, so it did not sit well when I did not respond to her. She walked by my desk, pointed at the utility closet, and in a stern voice said, "Now!" motioning for me to join her in the closet to hash things out. I responded, "I do not think that is a good idea!" to which she replied, "It was not a question!" I reluctantly got up and obliged.

My boss immediately began to berate me in anger and I couldn't hold my composure any longer with my emotional state. We screamed at each other but I have no regrets. By the end of our argument, I think she understood to the best of her ability, but someone who is solely career-focused can only comprehend so much. After our shouting match, she allowed me to leave. At that point, I had no idea if I would be able to keep my position, and for the rest of my time at that company, I walked on eggshells whenever I needed to ask for time off.

One day after I arrived home after a long day at work and after picking up the kiddos from daycare, Steve greeted me at the front door by saying, "Please do not be mad at me."

All I could say was, "What is wrong?"

He replied, "I told {major national news channel} to scram today." He continued, "I had just come out of dialysis, and they had called me multiple times while I was in there. I did not feel well, and I just wanted to get home to take a nap, but they would not leave me alone. When I finally picked up the phone, the producer was rude since I could not give them a time when we could do an interview because I needed to discuss it with you first. So, I told them to scram. Are you mad?"

That did not upset me one bit but rather made me proud of Steve for standing up for himself and his health. That is a trait I admire about Steve; he is unafraid to stand up for his family and does not care what others might think, other than me. He always wants to make sure we are both on the same page and desires for me to be proud of him, which I am…so proud!

That led to us having a long conversation about what our boundaries would be with the media since we could not possibly respond to all of the requests for interviews, let alone acquiesce to all of them. This upset some people, and a lot of them did not understand or respect that Steve was still sick and did not feel up to being on every podcast and radio station from here to Kalamazoo. We also discussed completely shutting off our phones and ignoring it all until it blew over, but we both felt that good could come from our story being shared if we got to control the narrative and elevate a message of hope and living kidney donation. Steve and I agreed we would take it one step at a time.

My number one priority has always been my family, but the fear of losing my job was always nudging me in the back of my head because my income was what kept our family afloat. We were drowning in medical bills. I went above and beyond at work, often going in early and staying late, working overtime, and if ever I needed to take off to take Steve to the hospital, I made up those hours later in the week. On dialysis days, I dreaded conversations with my supervisor if I needed to leave work early for something. I tried to hide all my stress about work from Steve because I did not want him to feel like he was a burden.

We interviewed with *Inside Edition* one day during the work week, and I remember asking my employer if we could use a conference room to do one of the interviews. I had been working so many hours that I would not have had the time to go home on my lunch break for the interview and come back to work. Thankfully they allowed it. I saved every single vacation day for Steve's hospital stays. He and I often joked about how they needed to offer hospital time shares or dedicate a wing of the hospital to us because of how often we were there. We called it "our home away from home." Some of the doctors and nurses felt like family to us. I would walk around the hospital halls in my house shoes and pajama pants, and everyone knew us by name.

We did interviews around my work schedule. There were local radio in-station interviews before work, written article interviews over the phone during lunch breaks, and podcasts and radio interviews all over the country after work. My Facebook message inbox held hundreds of messages from people, literally all over the world, saying they were praying for us and were inspired by our story. The exposure and well-wishes were humbling but also overwhelming. The media did a great job keeping us busy between the time we found out I was a match until I was finally approved to donate.

I had not been officially approved to donate yet so that weighed on my mind with all of the stories being shared about us and about how I was going to save my husband's life. Believe me, I had every intention to, but I also had to be cleared medically to donate. Just because we were a match did not mean that I could donate. Every interview we did I reminded Steve that we needed to reiterate that I still had medical testing to be done. I did not want anyone to feel misled if, for any reason, I was not approved. All the attention felt like I had tons of people peeping through my windows on a daily basis, and all with their expectations of me donating. I never put pressure on myself because it's what I wanted to do, but the pressure of letting people down, especially Steve, was suffocating.

By Steve

JUST BREATHE

The next few days were a whirlwind and we could not keep up with the insanity of going viral. One might say it's absolute chaos, but that is an extreme understatement. My dialysis treatments could not stop during this mayhem. As I walked into my next appointment some of the nurses who had seen us on television and the internet greeted me with big smiles. They shared how moved they were by the video and that it made them cry. Other dialysis patients were stopping me to offer their congratulations on the great news. It really hit me when my fellow patients were cheering about my good news because these were people who had been fighting for their lives and had been dealing with dialysis for decades but had not received their miracle. It made me feel horrible flashing my gift of life in front of them, and it also made me question whether or not Heather and I should be so accepting of the platform we had been given.

As the week went along, we were featured on just about every national news source from ABC, NBC, CBS, Fox, CNN, and even ESPN. Major League Baseball had reached out for a story and since my love for the game is immense, it meant the world to have their attention! After that we had feature stories in *Sports Illustrated*, *Southern Living*, *LAD Bible*, *PEOPLE*, and *Yahoo! News*. We even caught the attention of a famous actor and singer.

Only a few days after first going viral, things had become overwhelming for us. So my friend Chad from the American Kidney Fund offered to help. He said they would handle all of our calls and filter through the chaos before reaching out to us. Shortly after that, Chad called, and I could sense the excitement in his voice. He asked me if we would like to be on a talk show. "YES! We would love to!" The producer from the talk show, *Harry*, wanted to speak with us about being on the show. I called Heather the second I hung up with Chad and told her the big news.

She responded with, "Harry who?"

I replied, "Harry Connick, Jr., you know, the singer and actor from the movie *Independence Day!*"

She had the best hopelessly romantic reply…"Oh! The guy from *Hope Floats!*" Without hesitation, Heather said, "Yes, let's do it!" Her excitement had me even more thrilled. I had dreamed of being on a talk show as a child, so another dream was about to come to fruition.

After connecting with the producer and providing all the necessary information about our appearance, if we chose to accept, the producer told us they wanted to have us on the show two times, once before the transplant via Skype, and then again post-transplant in the studio in New York City. How much better could this get? I could not wait to tell Heather that the show would be flying us to New York City, and provide transportation and hotel accommodations! Besides living out a dream, the most important part of the experience would be sharing our story on a national scale and in-studio.

About a week or so after the phone call from Harry Connick, Jr.'s producer, we learned more about the talk show business and how it works. We had another talk show offer from a brand-new talk show that was going to begin shooting in Nashville. Their producer attempted to woo us to be on their show instead of being on *Harry*. We went back and forth between both show producers, and they each advised it was our call and to do what was best for us. We listened to the opportunities with both shows and made our final decision. I let the producer of the new Nashville talk show know that we decided to do the *Harry* show, but we appreciated her offer and interest in our story. She immediately became snippy and said she could not believe I would turn down my home state's show and proceeded to tell me all we would miss out on. Once I hung up, I knew we had made the right decision based on her less-than-desirable response. I also took her attitude as a harsh reminder that many media outlets saw our story as a way to increase their stats on social media, and they did not truly care about us as people. Thankfully that didn't include all media because we have made some dear friends that we have kept to this day.

Various other offers came for radio shows, podcasts, and other interviews, but we declined. I don't think the media understood that I was still sick, on dialysis, and still dealing with kidney failure. This meant I simply did not have the energy to say yes to all the requests. Heather and I talked about making sure we put ourselves, our family, and our health first. We wanted to accommodate as many media requests as possible, but also to not be afraid to say no to some of them. We appreciated all the publicity, but the *Harry* show had won our hearts. Harry Connick, Jr., had a great role in *Independence Day*, and his music was remarkable. Heather loved his music from the movie *When Harry Met Sally*, plus he was easy on the eyes and typically a favorite for the females.

The day had finally arrived for us to get on a Skype call with Harry for our first appearance on his show. The producer had let us know ahead of time what questions would likely be asked, and we gave her our answers so she could filter through them and let us know what sounded the best and what we could say or not say. There was enough preparation beforehand to ensure a good conversation but also enough leeway to maintain a more open dialogue instead of sounding robotic and rehearsed.

We were connected to the studio and could see everything going on live to prepare for the show, including the audience coming in and what they were being told. We were overjoyed to be a part of it, even if we were remote for the first appearance! Heather and I watched in fascination as the band prepped and practiced, the lights and many cameras were carefully placed, and people with headsets were scrambling about. The only time I had witnessed this kind of marvelous undertaking was at Disney World while they prepared to start a show and gave the audience an idea of what to expect. This show was the real deal, and they taped *Harry* in front of a live studio audience at CBS. No corners were cut, nor sacrifices made for the entire production. The *Harry* show was top of the line. As we observed from our kitchen, we both could not help but think to ourselves why we were there. How were two people from East Tennessee, who lived a simple life and quiet life, on this national network talk show? We had a difficult time comprehending how our story drew so much attention and why it seemed to have spread like wildfire.

As we silently waited for the show to start, we got a call from the producer letting us know we were watching the show live via Skype. She told us Harry would be coming onto the set in a few moments and that we would be able to see and hear him. She also advised us when we would be able to talk, and what our cue would be. Harry finally introduced us to the audience, and there we were, live on his talk show, chatting back and forth with this incredible singer and actor. Our nerves were rattled, but I don't think it came off that way during the interview. We were quick with our answers, carried on a great conversation, and even made Harry and the audience laugh. Harry asked us both about the day we learned Heather was a match, and he also asked about the status of the transplant. Once the interview came to an end, Harry announced to the audience that we would be back on the show again after the operation, but in the studio that time.

When we closed our computers, we both felt it went well, but we would not know for sure until it aired. The show has a live studio audience for recording, but they did not stream it live on television. We eagerly awaited for the day our episode aired. I sat in my dialysis chair as the show came on that morning. Since we knew I would be at dialysis when it aired, I set the television up to record the episode so we could watch it when we got home. To my surprise, just about every television at the dialysis center had on CBS. My heart raced in disbelief that our story was about to be shared with my dialysis warriors. Our segment came on towards the end of the episode, and there we were, my wife and I, on national television and for everyone in the dialysis center to see. I slumped down into my chair and slightly covered my face from embarrassment. I looked around and noticed a few people looking over at me, then at the television, back to me, and then back to the television. Some of the nurses came over and congratulated me on the story, but other than that, nobody said anything to me, which I didn't mind because, for whatever reason, I felt a little embarrassed and shy about the whole thing.

When I finished my session and was walking out of the clinic, a patient came up to me. He was an elderly man, and I had seen him most days, but since his chair was on the other side of the room, we never chatted. He grabbed my arm as I walked by, looked up at me, and said, "Son, please keep going and continue to be the voice for those who do not have one." He then let go of my arm and walked away. I kept on walking and burst into tears when I got into my car. Did I just get introduced to my purpose? Was this confirmation we had made the right choice by accepting our platform and using it to try and help others? All of these questions were racing through my head.

I couldn't wait to tell Heather what the elderly man had said. That evening, over dinner, we talked about our appearance on national television and how cool it was talking with Harry Connick, Jr., We were both happy with the show and looking forward to going to New York City to meet him in person. After that conversation, I brought up what happened at the dialysis clinic that morning and how it hit my heart. I told her the show was on every television set in dialysis and how the gentleman stopped me when I was leaving and told me to keep being a voice for others. Heather seemed emotionally struck by his words too. Sometimes this type of exposure can make you fall into a trap of doing things for the wrong reasons, so we wanted to always make sure awareness and helping others was the gasoline to our purpose. Hearing those words from the man outside of dialysis provided us a sigh of relief in knowing we made the right decision in accepting the platform.

Chapter 26

By Steve

WHAT IS YOUR FAVORITE CARD?

E veryone sitting in a dialysis chair has the opportunity to inspire others by sharing their story. We each have a story, and every story has an audience, whether it's ten or ten million people. I am glad we shared our story with the world, but with that exposure comes negative people. Strangers made the meanest comments about us, despite the fact that they did not know us at all. We were taken aback that people were saying some of the meanest things you could imagine. This rudeness hurt us, and we took it very personally at first. We were told to just ignore the threats and hateful comments, but we struggled. Celebrities are used to dealing with these types of things, but we come from a smaller city and a simpler life where people do not talk to one another like that.

We were blessed to have garnered several relationships with people who spend time in the public eye, and they shared their wisdom and helped us get through it. To this day, we will never understand why some people were so mean to us over a video of a wife telling her husband she was donating her kidney to him. The good news is that for every negative comment or person we encountered, we received a thousand kind comments. It took a little bit, but we learned to ignore the haters and unhappy people and to focus on our purpose instead. We did not allow them to ruin the beauty of the moment God had made for us.

More opportunities came about for us to share our story. We were heading to Atlanta for a Braves baseball game, and I remembered that a gentleman from CNN had reached out to us a while back and asked if we were ever in town to let him know. So I decided to reach out to him, and I'm glad I did because he invited us to come to the CNN studio that day for an interview. We didn't expect this and had not packed the right clothes for an interview. So we stopped and bought clothes that were more appropriate for television. This unexpected opportunity thrilled us, and when we reached CNN in downtown Atlanta, we did what every tourist would do…we took photos everywhere. CNN headquarters has a remarkably interesting building with a food court and shopping in the downstairs area, which features a wide-open view up to the glass ceiling. You could see people walking along the railing of each floor, all for things on CNN.

We had a few moments to kill before our meeting, so we got some food and looked around. We went into a sports store that sold all things Atlanta Braves, Atlanta Falcons, Atlanta Hawks, and numerous other collegiate merchandise. The man working the register asked us if we needed any help, and our conversation led to him asking where we were from and what brought us to CNN. When I shared why we were there, he became excited and said he knew exactly who we were. He had seen our story all over the internet and loved following me on social media because he, too, collected baseball cards. How amazing that this guy, that we had never met before, knew who we were and told me things he had seen me post on the internet. This was not the first time strangers had said they knew who we were, but it never became normal for us to accept strangers knowing who we were in public. It happened just days after the video had gone out on the internet. We were out for dinner with friends, and I noticed a few people kept looking over at us. I did not think much of it, other than they were just people-watching. As we were leaving, we noticed there was a crowd of about ten people standing right outside of the doors to the restaurant, and when we walked out, they all came over to us. One lady asked if we were the kidney transplant couple from the video on the internet. Heather and I blushed and told her yes, we were. They were so kind, and they all shook our hands and told us how our story touched them. Meeting those sweet strangers turned out to be a memory we will never forget. Their kind words meant the world to us both and played a big part in our accepting that our story was making a wonderful positive impact.

Another time someone recognized me in public was at a local baseball card shop. The employee working that day, Jimmy, greeted me, and we began talking about baseball and the hobby of collecting cards. While we were chatting, the phone rang, and Jimmy went in the back to answer it. When he came back he said he had an odd question to ask me and proceeded to explain that the owner of the store was on vacation and just checked the surveillance camera. He said the phone call was him asking if I was the guy in the baseball card video with his wife. I could not help but smile in disbelief and told him yes. How crazy, I thought, but it made me smile as I walked to my car because people were recognizing me because of something my selfless wife had done.

One of the most exciting interviews we had the honor of doing was through ESPN. A producer had emailed me asking if Heather and I would like to be interviewed live on *SportsCenter* one morning. Are you serious?! I had played basketball my entire life and every player dreamed of being featured on *SportsCenter* for an amazing play they made. I achieved the goal of being on *SportsCenter* due to my crying in a video that seemed to impact the nation. Not quite my most athletic play, but it was the greatest moment of my life. We were told our segment would be filmed in the University of Tennessee football facility. I had an idea so I reached out to our friends at the American Kidney Fund. I offered for Heather and me to wear their shirts during the interview if they wanted to send us some. They happily obliged, so we wore American Kidney Fund shirts on television as a way to help bring awareness to this amazing kidney disease charity.

We arrived at the football facility, and they took us into the studio that had a large camera set up with two taller chairs directly in front of it. The kind gentleman who helped us get set up also helped calm our nerves. We were placed in our seats and given microphones that were connected to our phones. We would not be able to see the person interviewing us, but we could hear everything through the earpiece. As we waited for the interviewer on ESPN to begin talking to us, all I could hear in my earpiece was silence. Then Heather began talking, but I could not hear anybody on the other side. My heart raced as I realized there was a technical difficulty and I needed to get the attention of the man behind the camera. Heather turned to me after everybody must have realized the issue, and she said to me, "He wants to know how you are doing?" She said it in a manner as if I were hard of hearing and not just my earpiece malfunctioning. Thankfully they went to a commercial break quickly to try to fix the technical mishap.

We came back on the air and everything worked perfectly. I pinched myself because we were on *SportsCenter* doing a live national interview with Will Reeve, the son of Superman, Christopher Reeve. Heather did an amazing job, and everything went great until the very last question of the interview. Will asked me, "So, Steve, what is your favorite card in your collection?" Without hesitation, I blurted out the very first card that came to mind, the 1989 Upper Deck Ken Griffey, Jr., rookie card. I followed this answer up by saying how easy of an answer that was. At this time, I hear Will laughing, Heather is hitting my arm and laughing, and I am sitting there clueless as to why the answer was being mocked. After we went off the air, we continued talking with Will, and he immediately said to me, "Steve! I just lobbed you a beachball to hit a home run with your wife on television and you missed!" Then, like a cold wind punching you across the face as you walk outside in the middle of a blizzard, I realized what had just happened. I should have said the card my wife made me, the card that announced she was saving my life, the card that was the reason we were even on television that day. Needless to say, to this day, Heather does not believe me when I tell her that her card is my favorite of all time.

When I got to work later that day, quite a few people poked fun and messed with me because of my unfortunate answer. More people were watching *SportsCenter* that morning than I had thought. Months later when I ran into some people I knew who worked in the Tennessee Athletics Department, they brought up that *wrong* answer I gave on national television. One friend of mine said he was in his office watching *SportsCenter,* and when he heard my answer, he almost spit out his coffee. I suppose I have no excuses for not saying the card Heather made for me, but the fact remains that the 1989 Upper Deck Ken Griffey, Jr., rookie card is a legendary card to me.

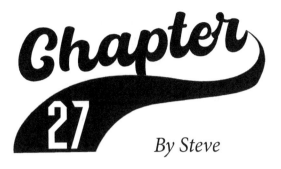

Chapter 27

By Steve

IT'S YOUR TURN TO GET CAMERA-READY

A ll of the commotion and emotion from the reveal of Heather telling me she was a match masked the reality of the life-changing operation we were about to go through. I will never forget, a month or so after the video went viral, we were eating in a Cracker Barrel and talking about the whirlwind we had just experienced when we both realized it tainted our future reality. We had a very serious surgery on the horizon, and not just for one of us…for both of us. We had been so consumed with media requests, interviews, dialysis, and the emotional high of knowing the surgery was happening that we lost track of actually talking about the surgery. We needed to slow down, step back, and talk about the operation that was only a few weeks out.

We had one more interview commitment with CNN that we ended up doing and a tour of the new Atlanta Braves ballpark with the former Braves World Series-winning pitcher, Greg McMichael. This opportunity felt like a homerun since we are huge Braves fans. We had great seats for the game in addition to the personal tour and front row seats on the field for batting practice. Our two foster babies were with us at the time, so we were excited about showing the two-year-old a professional baseball game. We had also just learned that the children would be moving to Florida soon to live with their grandparents. This trip was also a celebration of love and appreciation for their being in our lives. As foster parents, it is painful to see kids leave your home, especially when you brought them home from the hospital as babies and loved them so much. At the same time, seeing them go with their family is a blessing, and in my heart, I knew it was the best thing for them.

We arrived in Atlanta at the CNN Headquarters and were led up to the studios by the gentleman who was interviewing us, Don Riddell. We immediately fell in love with Don and his personality, his genuine care for us, his accent, and the fact that he called me "mate." A lot of media people are just doing their job; they interview you, and then you go on your way, which is fine; but we connected with Don on a deeper level and even got to have lunch together later that day. We could feel his concern for us; we knew he was interested in our story. Our interview was with CNN International, World Sport, which provided a huge opportunity to make an impact globally. We were sent to a green room where we got ready, and then we were each taken for makeup and hair to get ready for the show. This was surreal to us as it was our first time in a green room and being involved with makeup and hair. Needless to say, it took them quite a while to get me television-ready, but Heather looked amazing and ready to shine on television. We enjoyed the interview, and since Heather already filled you in on all the details in a previous chapter, there is no need for me to explain it…wink, wink!

With our interview obligation under our belts, we checked into our hotel and then headed to the ballpark. The vibe inside the Braves new ballpark felt amazing, and we were happy it was also family-friendly. There were places to shop and eat, and places for the kids to play and interact with the mascots. The music playing in the area around the stadium set the tone for the special feeling you get being at the "ol' ballpark." We met up with our friend, Greg McMichael, and as a bonus, also got to meet his friend and former Atlanta Braves catcher, Javy Lopez. We all chatted it up and took a bunch of photos.

Travis, our two-year-old foster child, had the time of his life, and we bonded even more with him, even if it was our last hoorah as a family. Greg gave us a tour of every part of the new stadium, from the expensive suites, the player tunnel, and the kid's area in the outfield, to taking us down onto the field. Greg is a wonderful human and so sweet that he pushed Travis around in his stroller during the tour. We felt his sincerity for us and our foster kids, which made the day even more special and a memory etched in our hearts forever. Greg debuted in 1993 for the Atlanta Braves as a rookie and had a wonderful season. He finished runner-up in the National League Rookie of the Year vote, second only to the winner, Mike Piazza… yes, the future Hall of Fame catcher for the Dodgers, Mike Piazza, so it was quite an accomplishment. We love Greg and his family and are forever grateful for what he did for us that day.

Chapter 28
By Steve and Heather

A CALM THAT SURPASSES ALL UNDERSTANDING

Heather

September 26th, 2017, arrived, and it was a morning we were dreading. Our foster children, that we had in our home for eight months, were leaving for Florida. We brought Kayleigh home from the hospital at the age of three weeks, and Travis was just two years old. Those tender ages allow you to fall in love with kids so easily, and having to let them go devastated us. Our hearts broke as we imagined how much we were going to miss them and wondered if we would ever see them again. We had met the grandparents several times and felt they were great people, so we were happy they were going to be with them but sad it had to be so far away. The foster agency instructed us to bring boxes of their belongings with them to daycare that morning, and they would come to pick them up and take the kids to meet up with the grandparents in Atlanta for the drop-off. This meant when we said goodbye to them at daycare, that it was the final goodbye. We had our photo taken with the kids one last time and then managed to pull ourselves away before they could see our tears. The floodgates opened as soon as Steve and I made it to the car. The pain of having to look a child in his eyes and tell him bye-bye, knowing you would not be coming back, tore me up. I had the feeling Travis knew something wasn't right as he acted out, not wanting us to leave, for the first time. Normally, he would run off and play, but that particular morning, he clung to us, hoping we wouldn't leave. Thinking about the desperation in that little boy's eyes is what makes me cry to this day.

Steve

We decided to go to the closest Chick-fil-A and cry it out in a booth in the corner for a while before even thinking about eating. We reminisced about all of the fond memories we had of raising our first baby together, having a two-year-old hug us and call us mommy and daddy for the first time, and just watching them grow. Many people say they cannot foster because they want to avoid any such pain, but I would tell them that when it hurts so much to see them go, you know in your heart that you helped them so much by being there for them and because you connected. It is when you do not cry or show emotion when a child leaves that you should be concerned. Having your heart broken in that manner is a sign you helped fill their life with love while they were with you. It is the child's journey, and you were blessed to be a part of that whether it be a few nights or a few years.

Once we gathered ourselves and ate, we tried to refocus our attention on the transplant that was just two days away, and we were leaving the next day for Nashville. There was no question we were more emotional about the children leaving than the operation at this point. I would have traded the transplant operation to have the kids with us a little longer in a heartbeat. However, God had all of us on our journey that day, and He needed us to move on to the next phase, as hard as it was.

After our tears had dried and our prayers had been said, we packed our final things, and we were in the car on our way to Nashville for a kidney transplant. We were focused and counting our blessings because we were on our way to undergo an amazing surgery

– my wife was giving me an organ to save my life. The three-hour drive included us talking, listening to music, laughing, telling stories, and every so often talking about the surgery. I opened up about my emotions, especially those of nervousness, but Heather kept her thoughts to herself.

We talked about how multiple media outlets had been requesting to talk to us before the operation, which seemed asinine to us because we had to be there at **5 A.M.** and most likely would not feel like talking to anybody. Vanderbilt's media department had the great idea to have one of their people talk to us along with a camera guy, but we dictated when we wanted to talk about or when it was time to shift focus. They were then in charge of the footage and "B-Roll" and sent it out to the various news agencies to use. This worked out very well, and we were glad Vanderbilt stepped up to help protect us from potential chaos the morning of our transplant.

As we lay on the bed in our hotel room, we both browsed our phones and did whatever we could to stay preoccupied. After a while, I turned to Heather and I asked if she had a full understanding of what was going to happen the next morning. Why? She was calmer than anybody I had ever seen in her position awaiting a major surgery. I will never forget her response to my question, "I know this is what God needs me to do for my husband, so I feel very calm about my decision and tomorrow's operation." Her response and overall calmness blew me away, almost to the point of making me wonder if I was overreacting to it all. I had always been inspired by Heather and her ability to take moments one step at a time and rationally deal with them, and here she was doing it again. Heather and I are opposites in many ways, but I believe that is why we work so well with together. Our deep respect for one another shines through whenever issues arise for either of us, and the other is always there with a cool head and ready to help the other. Seeing her calm nature about donating a body part to me made me feel better since my biggest fear with the operation was my wife's well-being. I did not want her to be in too much pain or experience any suffering. I had had numerous surgeries at this point in my life, so I was used to it, but this was her first major surgery.

I am pretty sure I didn't catch a wink of sleep that night since my mind kept thinking about Heather and my worry for her. This is why many dialysis patients will not ask a loved one to donate their kidney, because of the fear of their being hurt or injured long term. I knew I needed the operation and wanted it, but that didn't stop the battle between my heart and my mind. My brain was telling me I needed the kidney to live, and hopefully a long and fruitful life, but my heart was having a hard time allowing myself to be ok with her undergoing such a major surgery just for me.

I recall getting up in the middle of the night to use the bathroom, and I just sat there and cried. An array of emotions began coursing through my veins, and I did not want to wake Heather. I took myself out of the equation in which it was me who was being donated to, and I looked at our story from a distance. I watched some of the interviews we had done and tuned into the words Heather used to describe her decision. That's when it hit me, how lucky I was. I had married the most beautiful woman in the world, who had the largest heart and most caring soul I had ever met. She was so eager to get tested and to save my life. Think about that kind of selfless love. Imagine having a wife who would do anything it took to help her husband, sacrificing her own body, and giving an organ to him. How do you possibly show your highest gratitude for that?

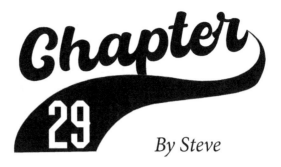

By Steve

FACTOID: I LOVE YOU FOR SAVING MY LIFE

After I calmed myself down, I did manage to get an hour or two of sleep before the alarm clock rang. We both got ready for the day in a silent manner, as if all thoughts and comments were sent telekinetically during this time. In our minds, we both knew what the other was thinking. We both had to take showers that morning using a special brand of anti-bacterial soap, but we could not use deodorant, hair products, or anything with a scent per our pre-operation instructions from Vanderbilt. Before leaving the room, we came together and grasped one another so tightly. It made perfect sense for us to slow-dance to our song before we left in case we didn't have time once we got to the hospital. Just like all the other times, we turned on Michael Bublé's "Everything" and held each other as tight as possible as we melted into the moment. We were about to head over to the hospital where my wife was going to save my life. This was not a metaphorical saving of life, but a literal saving with the donation of her kidney to me. We slowly danced and molded into one, just as we were about to become one again in that operating room. The song ended, and we kissed as if it were the last time we would kiss, then gathered our things, and we were out the door.

The car ride was once again quiet, and the interstate destitute that early in the morning, and it seemed as if God had cleared the way for us as we drove to our destiny. As we passed what few cars were on the interstate in the dark, I could not help but wonder if these people had any clue where our car was headed and why. Life goes by us in a tunnel of vision without a clue as to the beauty of life in the car next to you. The sun peaked out of the ground in the distance as we got closer to the hospital. The light of day presented itself as we were nearing the end of our darkness before the dawn of new life. We approached the hospital, where we had our car dropped off, and were immediately greeted by our Pastor, Wade Bibb. Pastor Bibb had been a mentor to me spiritually and as a life coach. He had been there for all of the difficult times and proved his love once again as he showed up to greet us. We hugged tightly, had a picture taken, and made our way into the hospital.

As we walked to the registration area, we were headed off by the media folks from Vanderbilt. They introduced themselves and gave a brief overview of what the interviews and filming would look like after we registered. At this point, Heather and I were both nervous and tired, so we were not sure that we wanted to talk to anybody. What motivated us to go through with filming was the idea that people could see what happens leading up to the transplant operation, and perhaps it could ease nerves for those in our shoes in the future. We made an effort to try and remember it was not always about us, no matter how much we wanted it to be or not to be at times.

They took us to a couch area in the lobby of the hospital, which also served as the waiting area before being called upstairs to prep for the operation. We were interviewed and asked questions about how we felt, about our viral video, and things we wanted others to know about how it felt to be receiving a kidney from my wife. The lady interviewing made us feel comfortable, and the cameraman was kind, so we felt good talking to them, even if we did not feel up to it. After about twenty minutes, we heard our names called. Our time had come – the moment we had been anticipating for months and that I had been waiting on for nearly fourteen years. The cameraman was instructed to follow us up and into prep to get footage and a "B-roll" for the story. This did feel awkward to both of us as we were basically in a movie being directed on what to do. Heather and I naturally held hands and this moment was no different. Our camera guy got ahead of us through a set of doors and told us to wait a few moments before walking through ourselves, so he could get the shot he wanted. We were taking the most important walk of our marriage which felt strange being followed by a camera.

On that walk to the prep room, while being directed, Heather and I carried on a beautiful conversation. We talked about our love, how we were genuinely about to become one, and how God was walking right there alongside us. Nerves, excitement, and quiet thoughts about each other's well-being tagged with us. We were walking down the hall to our new future. Within hours my entire life was about to change. Every moment in dialysis, every feeling of anger, sadness, disappointment, and depression was about to receive its final blow from the selflessness of my wife. They would not survive this operation. I cannot recall a moment where my heart was bursting with love as much as that moment. Just as we had during our first date, we were walking, and talking, and all I wanted to say to her was, "Factoid, I love you more than life itself. I love you for saving my life. I love you for loving me."

We arrived at the prep room and were both given our hospital gowns to put on. There were two beds with a curtain to separate for modesty and privacy, but we would have torn the curtain down if able. I wanted to be close to Heather the entire time. I did not want anybody sticking her with needles without me being right there to hold her hand. We hugged one another so many times that morning, but the final hug before retiring to our separate beds lasted the longest. I never wanted to let go, but for her to fulfill what she called God's request of her, I needed to let go.

They prepped Heather first by inserting the IV and putting a pain blocker into her abdomen. Luckily for me, I am tall, and on my tippy toes, I could watch over the curtain, and I reminded them to please be gentle and careful. It pained me when I heard her say "ouch" at times, but I knew she was in good hands and that I needed to lie down in my bed so they could begin my prep. After they had finished getting her IVs situated, they opened the curtain and put us side by side. I loved that they did this! They had given her something to calm her nerves at this point, so she was beginning to feel and act a little loopy. I knew I only had a few moments before she drifted away into la-la land. I told her again how much I loved her, and most importantly, I thanked her. All I could do right then was thank her and tell her how she had never looked more beautiful in all her life. I also had to have a little fun once her silly juice kicked in. I asked her trick questions about our foster kids, about things she said she had done or not done, but in Heather fashion, even with the silly juice, she still managed to be as sharp as a tack!

At last, the doctor came in and talked to her along with the anesthesiologist. It was time to roll her back for surgery. We were still holding hands as they began moving her bed and I could not let go. I begged them to allow her to stay one more minute, which they kindly obliged. I whispered how she was the most beautiful soul in the world, my guardian angel, and I thanked her once again for loving me so much that she would sacrifice her own body to save mine. I squeezed her hand, and like letting go of your favorite balloon as a child, I released her from my grip, and away she went. My stomach was in knots.

The nurses began my prep but they would not be taking me back for another hour and a half since they needed to remove Heather's kidney before I was put under. Lying there alone after they took her away was by far the longest hour and a half of my life. I longed to be in the operating room right next to her. All I could think about that entire time was whether or not they had begun taking the kidney out. Was she under enough anesthesia? What if she woke up? But, I knew God was with her in the operating room which was enough assurance for me. Eventually, the nurses gave me my dose of silly juice to calm my nerves, and I began melting into my pillow. After spending an eternity waiting, it was my turn to be taken back. Of course, I asked the surgeon about Heather first thing, and he told me she was doing great, and everything was going smoothly. He then explained how the handoff would work between operating rooms and the protocols in place for handling such a delicate organ. My showtime had begun. The sound of the brakes being taken off of the gurney echoed the beginning of a brand-new life, and I shivered with goosebumps. I had dreamt about this moment for a long time.

Once in the operating room, I remember it feeling so cold. Beeping noises filled the air, people walked around getting prepared, and then I heard the music playing. *Are they playing music*, I thought to myself. And it wasn't just any music, but great classic rock. For whatever reason this calmed me. Music had been there for me through dialysis and my anxiety as a child. Music, along with my wife, got me through some of the hardest times of my life, so how fitting that music greeted me to start my life-altering surgery. The medical team slid me onto the operating table and began hooking me up with various probes that measured my vitals. Things were moving quite quickly. Since I had experience as a patient in the operating room, I always found a way to lighten the mood. My favorite amusement and personal challenge was to see how high I could count before being knocked out, and I would let the anesthesiologist know my current record. Thirteen was my personal best at that time, so I informed him of this, and he seemed amused at my attempt to fight the anesthesia for as long as I could. He chuckled and explained the medicine had been undefeated, but he welcomed the challenge. I started my count as he inserted the anesthesia and began reminiscing quickly as I counted …1 …2 …3 …4 …5 … Images danced around in my head of meeting Heather for the first time, shaking hands for the first time, our first date, and how it all led to that moment. A spectacular vision. God knew the moment we laid eyes on each other in 2010, and on April 24th, 1985 the day that I was born, that this gift of life had been scheduled …6 …7 …8 …9 … God's destiny for us. …10 …11 …12 …13 …

My eyelids fluttered as they were waking up. I could hear the sound of beeps from a heart monitor acting as my alarm clock. As my vision finally cleared, and I was somewhat aware of where I was, I immediately began feeling this excruciating pain in my lower abdomen area. I remember a nurse quickly came over and offered to help me with the pain. I must have fallen back asleep moments later. The next time my eyes opened I was still in the same spot, but my transplant nephrologist, Dr. Heidi Schaefer, was standing there. A joyful sight. She asked me how I was feeling, and she later shared with me that I proceeded to ask her a question.

"So, does this mean I have to sit to pee now?"

After she stopped laughing, she informed me I could pee however I wanted, but it was not mandatory. I always enjoyed her sense of humor.

My new life had officially begun, but I had some serious recovery to get through before I could take full advantage of it. Looking back, I realized after I opened my eyes from my transplant, that my journey through kidney disease was no longer about me. I had made it through the operation most dialysis patients dream of. I was a fortunate one. This new life that so many others desired, a second chance, had just been handed to me. Aside from showing gratitude to my donor, I felt an obligation to use my gift as a way to help others find their second chance. So many dialysis patients would give anything to break the shackles and be in my position, pain, and all.

After a few minutes of fully coming out of the grogginess, I called my nurse over and told her I wanted to see my wife and needed to know how she was doing. How did her operation go? She informed me I could not see her at the time, but she had word Heather was doing fine and her operation went off without a hitch. Hearing those words helped to ease my heart of its anxiety and worry. I still needed to see for myself, to touch her, and to see her beautiful smile.

They eventually rolled me to a recovery room upstairs on the transplant floor. Heather was on that floor as well, which thrilled me. I needed to see her, but they said not until later that evening because she was still recovering like me. Heather's operation was much harder on her because a donor is losing a healthy organ, whereas the recipient is gaining what they need to make them better. Her recovery proved to be quite painful, and I am glad I did not know that at the time because I would have likely jumped out of my bed and gone to her aide immediately. Heather's room was on the completely opposite side of the floor as mine and there was purpose behind this decision. The transplant team wants you up and walking as soon as possible, so they knew the further apart we were, the more likely we would want to walk to one another. A brilliant plan, yet annoying.

I had a catheter in, staples running across my abdomen no shorter than six to eight inches, and I had a tube sticking out of my abdomen attached to a bag collecting blood and fluid. A recipe for misery. I vomited due to the pain, and I am sure I came across as a pain to those caring for me that first day. But then I heard a knock on my sliding door. A nurse I hadn't met yet had a big smile on her face and proclaimed I had a visitor. My mood flipped in an instant, and I sat up as much as I could. There she stood, being helped by a nurse arm in arm. Heather wore a surgical binder around her stomach as her hunched-over body moved ever so slowly towards me. The tears dropped from my face onto my hospital gown as I begged her to come closer. Heather couldn't hold back her floodgates at this point either. All of the emotions of excitement, the pain, and then not knowing for sure how the other was doing gushed into this epic moment of two hearts being reconnected. I kept asking Heather to bend over further to hug me, but her pain did not allow it so she sat in the chair at my side and did the next best thing… we held hands.

The imagery of that meeting in my hospital room, with the nurses joining us in tears of joy, would have beams of light shining down from Heaven had someone painted the picture. In our hearts, we both said, "I do," once more before setting sail on the voyage of our second chance for love.

Chapter 30

By Heather

I WOULD DO IT AGAIN IN A HEARTBEAT...

The beeping of our alarm awoke us from our thoughts. Our heads were resting on our hotel room pillows, but our eyes had been wide awake since we laid them down hours ago. Neither Steve nor I had ever fallen asleep that night because there were too many things to ponder, and we would both be taking a long-medicated nap very soon anyway. It was finally the day of surgery. I could feel the anxiousness radiating off of Steve, but I had never felt so calm. All my previous anxiety had been wrapped up in my feeling helpless, feeling like there was nothing I could do for my husband. But my time had arrived; I could finally shine and do something significant with the hope of making a difference for him. It brought me joy to be able to physically take on some of the pain of this disease for Steve. With every fiber of my being, I knew I was called to do this, and I had peace that everything would turn out ok. Even if there were complications, at least I knew I had done everything in my power.

We sat up; we were side by side on the edge of the hotel bed in silence, soaking in the gravity of this day. This was going to be a day we would remember forever. The emotions flooding our bodies could not have been more polar opposite, but that was us. I was the Yin to his Yang. We took turns having bad days. If one of us felt stressed or anxious, the other one would focus on being the rock and support. I knew today I had to be strong for Steve. After a few moments of silence, I turned my body toward his, put my arms around his shoulders, and placed my head on his chest. I prayed he could feel the peace that I felt; I hoped this embrace would let him know everything would turn out alright.

We got ready in silence and drove to Vanderbilt Transplant Center in the same silence. I think we just knew how the other was feeling, and nothing I said could change the nerves Steve had because they existed out of his love for me. His biggest concern was my well-being. Nothing could rattle the peace I felt in my decision or make me change my mind because of my love for him.

When we arrived at Vanderbilt Transplant Center we were greeted, before we even entered the automatic doors, by a friendly and familiar face. Our pastor and friend, Dr. Wade Bibb, had driven from Knoxville to Nashville exceedingly early that morning to see us through another milestone in our relationship. He had been there marrying us on our wedding day five years prior, and now he prayed over us as we "became one" for the second time. This occasion was even more momentous than the day we were married. Not all married couples will experience the closeness that we were about to embark on. After a quick prayer and hugs, we walked through the automatic glass doors. The steps that followed were a blur.

We were escorted through white halls to a pre-operative room and given the rundown of transplant surgeries. I then asked if I could use the restroom before they started to prep me. I went into the small bathroom attached to the pre-operative room, which was filled with family members, anesthesiologists, nurses, and techs. Of all the inopportune times, I had to poop which proved to be a challenging task. I remember trying to drown out the excited chatter directly outside the bathroom door when I heard a nurse knock, "Are you ok in there?" They probably thought I was having second thoughts, but I just really needed to poop. My nerves had been calm up until then because it felt so weird having an entire medical team waiting on you while you were just trying to take care of some business.

Once I finished my *number two*, I came out and met my anesthesiologist. He asked me if I wanted something to help me relax. I told him I felt at peace but why not? After receiving whatever drug he gave me, I felt my body melt into the gurney, my peripheral vision closed, and voices around me started to drown out. I could only focus on one thing at a time, and at that moment, it was on the instructions of the anesthesiologist. He drew the curtain between Steve and us for a little privacy, and then he explained how he was going to put this needle (he showed me the largest needle I had ever seen) into my abdomen and give me an injection that would numb it for 48 hours and make recovery a little easier. He explained it would feel like a rubber band snapping under my skin and it felt exactly like that, not too painful but just more uncomfortable.

I must have groaned when he put it in because Steve, at six feet and two inches, popped his head so quick over the curtain dividing us and begged, "Please don't hurt my wife." I could hear the anguish in his voice and knew he was struggling with the thought of me experiencing this pain for him. My surgeon walked in and asked if anyone wanted to say a quick prayer before they took me off to surgery. The emotions welled up inside of me as I was about to entrust myself and Steve to the medical team. Steve grabbed my hand, kissed me, and we said I love you, then they wheeled me to the operating room.

I woke up incredibly agitated. An overwhelming feeling came over me while in the recovery room, and I thought *I did not have to be strong anymore* – I had done all I could do. The excruciating pain I felt was almost a relief of sorts, because, for me, it represented the pain I had felt all along watching Steve suffer. Now, he was not alone in this fight or his pain. We were one. The previous weight on my shoulders had relocated into my abdomen.

My post-surgical distressed self couldn't shake being incredibly pissed…at, of all the random things I could have been pissed at, the air in the recovery room; the air felt stale, an assault on my senses, a rude awakening from a peaceful, medically induced nap that I was not yet prepared to wake up from. The stagnant, stinky, germ-filled hospital air suffocated my throat, although I couldn't choke. There were so many beeping noises, bright fluorescent lights, and medical smells bombarding my senses. I felt this throbbing pain in my abdomen and everything else around me, including the air, people, and inanimate objects, were all annoying the heck out of me. I just wanted to go back to sleep and wake up when the pain was gone.

A thin curtain separated me from my neighbor in recovery who had quite the voice. To me, her voice resembled nails on a chalkboard, although I imagine she was not the monster I made her out to be in my head. At that minute, though, I was not a very pleasant person, and I wished she did not exist. How could she be so chipper? Had she not just come out of surgery too? Yes, she had hip replacement surgery. I heard it all as her screechy and happy-go-lucky self, vocalized incessantly about her hip, and her dogs whom she referred to as her "furry children" (this got under my skin, probably because I had just said goodbye to my foster babies two days prior and I had not had time to grieve that immense loss), her recovery plans, her sister, her house, her hopes, wishes, and dreams, and everything else under the sun. Why was she in such a good mood? Why would she not shut up? More importantly what drugs was she on, where was my nurse, and could I have what she was having – PLEASE?

At that time, *Ms. Happy Clappy's* nurse came by and offered her some more painkillers. Her response: she was fine, not in any pain at all, but why not if she wanted to stay ahead of the pain? Then shortly after, my nurse came by and offered me some medicine. Thank goodness, *finally, I will get some relief,* I thought. As I used all my energy to lift my head high enough not to choke on the pills but not high enough to cause my abdominal muscles to be engaged, I asked what he was giving me. "Tylenol."

Regular old Tylenol. Tylenol – what you take when you have a mild headache or fever. NOT what I imagine you would take when a FREAKING ORGAN HAD JUST BEEN REMOVED FROM YOUR BODY. He walked away. An ORGAN, my kidney, had just been removed from my body. *Tylenol? Really?* I guess the giant needle they put into my abdomen before surgery was supposed to block the nerves for at least 48 hours, so I was not supposed to be in pain. But I was – in excruciating pain. Normally, I am a very pleasant, patient, and kind person, but I wanted to pick a fight with the air around me and the happy lady behind that very thin curtain. For whatever reason, the pain blockers were working just as well for me as that thin curtain was working at blocking out my obnoxious hospital roommate.

Not soon enough, they moved me up to the transplant recovery room to heal in peace without a roommate and with my very own air to breathe. However, the pain continued pounding in my gut like the bass in a nightclub on a Saturday night. It would not ease up or go away. Finally, a resident doctor came to visit me. He found me almost wrapped up like a taco in my hospital bed. I looked extremely uncomfortable because I was! He asked if he could adjust my bed to lay me flatter, and I begged, "No, please do not move the bed. If the bed is flattened at all my body is going to rip in half." I couldn't take the agony within me. He seemed very concerned as he examined me and promised I would be given something for the pain soon. As he walked out of the room, he stopped, turned around, and empathetically asked, "If you knew what you know now, would you still do it?"

I sobbed from my internal torment as I managed a swift smile for a second and shouted, "Yes, I would! This is the best thing I have ever done. If I had another kidney, I would give it away to a stranger if I could! I would do it again in a heartbeat." Tears of compassion filled his eyes. I think feelings of relief came to him that his Hippocratic oath to do no harm was not in jeopardy partaking in living donation after I answered his question. I thought to myself, *this young man has compassion and empathy, he will be an excellent doctor one day!* I wish I had told him so.

That evening, after a dose of pain medicine, a nurse aide helped me stand for the first time after surgery, and I told her I wanted to see Steve. She helped walk me and my IV pole down the hall to the other side of the transplant floor where my husband was recovering. That walk felt like a pilgrimage to the other side of the world after just learning to walk again. I asked myself, "Is my body going to rip in half from this grueling trek?" Whatever the consequence, I thought it was worth it. As I approached the sliding glass doors to Steve's room, a nurse pulled back a privacy curtain as she announced to Steve, "You have a visitor!"

Tears filled Steve's eyes immediately upon seeing me. I had on two hospital gowns, one on the front and one backward, covering up my backside for modesty, and I had a binder on my belly that I'm pretty sure was the only thing holding in my insides. I could not stand upright if I had tried. Then the first thing my husband said was, "You are so beautiful!" I stood beside his bed, gazing at him in awe. He looked well. I had not seen him looking well in so long.

"I need to hold you, to hug you!"

I knew he wanted to make sure I was okay, but I replied, "I cannot bend over. Hug my hand!" I put my hand in his, and he squeezed it as a nurse pulled up a chair for me to sit in to be closer to him. We just sat there and looked at each other, stroking each other's arms, hands, cheeks. Steve later told me that seeing me entering his room was like reliving our wedding day. I was wearing a gown, being escorted to him, looking more beautiful than I had ever looked before, in his eyes. I thought he was so sweet; I was not looking my best, but I knew from his sincerity that I truly was the most beautiful to him at that moment. He did not see a hospital gown and my messy hair. All he saw was my soul. Steve loved me, for me. He loved all of me, completely, imperfections and all.

The next day it was my turn for a visitor, so Steve took that lengthy stroll across the transplant floor to see me. He arrived at my door beaming, and my heart thumped with excitement! I urged him to sit down and rest when he came in, but instead, he did a little twirl dance for me. I tried not to laugh as I clutched my belly at my incision site because it hurt to laugh. I could not help but giggle as he flashed his booty cheeks out of the back of his parting hospital gown. Joy radiated from my husband which filled my heart with so much joy. We both had a long road to recovery, but I knew we were going to be okay.

ACT 3

Chapter 31

By Steve

WELCOME TO NYC AND CBS STUDIOS!

The transplant team didn't release us until the following Monday. They rolled us down to the front door, and we left the hospital the same way we arrived…together, facing a new dawn, a new day, and a new opportunity. The sun seemed to shine brighter, the air smelled sweeter, and my heart felt warmer. We headed to our hotel room instead of home because we had to spend the next week or so near Vanderbilt for post-op appointments.

Recovery in the hotel was not ideal, but we had one another and just enough strength to be there for each other. Every day seemed to tease us as we thought we had regained our strength, but after showering and putting clothes on, we found ourselves exhausted and back in bed. The outpouring of love we received while in the hospital touched us deeply. A news channel came to my room to interview me once I felt well enough. We had a photographer and journalist from *The Tennessean*, Nashville's most popular newspaper, come by one day and speak with us for about an hour. Aside from that, we had privacy in our hotel room while we recovered. We were not up for visitors and just wanted to be to ourselves. I remember receiving a message online asking me if I had seen Knoxville's newspaper, *The*

News Sentinel. I had not, and they proceeded to send me a message with a photo. The entire front page featured a photo and news spread of me and Heather. In large black letters at the top, it read, "Perfect Match," with a photo of us taken at the hotel just days before. It shocked us that we had made the front page of Knoxville's largest newspaper!

At my one-week follow-up visit to Vanderbilt, Heather and I met with my nephrologist Dr. Heidi Schaefer. We chatted for a few minutes about the excitement of finally having had the transplant and the resulting media coverage. Then Dr. Heidi Schaefer asked if I had any concerns. I said, I did have one thing I was a little concerned about. I lifted my shirt and showed her my drainage tubes and explained that occasionally it still leaks, mostly if I laugh really hard. After glancing at the drain and noting that it did not appear to be infected and was not oozing an abnormal amount for this stage of recovery, she sarcastically quipped "put a maxi pad on it, Steve!" to which Heather immediately burst out "ha!" When they finally cleared us to go home, we were beyond ready to be back in our house and our comfy bed. Our bodies were exhausted still, and we needed some time to get adjusted to life again. The amazing thing about the transplant was that within hours of the operation, the medical team said the color of my face had changed, and I looked healthier. The kidney began working immediately which blew my mind.

We had been home about a week when we received a phone call from Harry Connick, Jr.'s producer. They wanted us to fly to New York City for the in-studio portion of the show at CBS, but we worried it was too soon since we would be just five weeks post-transplant. As the date came closer, Heather and I realized we would be able to make the trip with permission from both of our teams at Vanderbilt. They approved us, and our trip to CBS studios in New York City was booked. We had another call with the producer to answer a ton of questions that would be vetted and then the questions with the best answers would be used on the show. After this interview, they sent us a script with the questions Harry was going to ask us in order and the answers they wanted us to respond with based on our prior answers. Technically there is a script for a talk show appearance, but seeing that we essentially wrote the script, it was still just a conversation.

The big day came and reality hit that our trip to be on a talk show was happening! We arrived at the airport early to make sure we did not miss our flight. We hoped our appearance would inspire at least one person to register to be a donor or a living donor.

On Monday, November 6th, we got off the plane in New York City. The producer told us a driver would be waiting for us, so as we came down an escalator, we saw a gentleman in a fancy suit, sunglasses, and an electronic pad that read, *Winfree*. How cool! He led us to an elegant, black SUV, with tented windows. Inside, we had drinks and snacks for us to enjoy as we headed towards our hotel. We were told by the producer that the driver had already been tipped, so we just needed to sit back, enjoy the ride, and take in the sights of our first time in New York City together.

We loved our driver and his candor with us as we made our way to the hotel. He took us through Queens and eventually across the Queensborough Bridge that we had heard about in the opening of *The King of Queens* for so many years. We stared out the window in awe of the amazing view of the city. So many sites felt familiar everywhere we looked since we had probably seen them in a show or movie. We were two regular people from East Tennessee being treated like rock stars, driving through New York City in a tinted-out, black SUV. We explained to the driver why we were there and he loved our story, and then we learned he was the driver who picks up all celebrities and guests on the *Harry* show. Wow!

We arrived at our hotel, got checked in, and then had a few minutes to relax before heading out to walk through New York City. We had a quick lesson on how to use the subway system because we had to be at the Topps Headquarters in a short amount of time. When we arrived at Topps, they sent us up an elevator that opened up to the lobby, and we were greeted by our tour guide, Susan. She worked in the marketing department and had been our contact from the beginning. She introduced us to everybody there, including the CEO. They all treated us so well, and we will never forget the CEO telling us he thought our video was a marketing piece put together by his team from their custom cards division because it was so beautiful and perfect. How surreal to meet the CEO of the company that created baseball cards from my childhood. I was a kid in a candy store, to say the least.

Once the tour ended, Susan gave us goody bags filled with some incredible boxes of baseball cards and a special baseball bat. We were worried about being let on the subway with a bat but soon realized we fit in simply fine. The trip had just begun and was already both amazing and overwhelming, and we were blessed to be living the experience. That night, we spent hours going over the script, getting ready for our national television appearance the next morning, and then called it a night.

Our alarm went off, and we got ready and put on our outfits, which had been approved by the producers prior to us leaving home. It was very chilly that morning in New York City, so we had to bundle up for our short walk to CBS Studios. We knew we were in the right place when we saw a large marquee that read, *Harry*, with a picture of Harry Connick, Jr., Since we were technically tourists, we stopped and took photos, but unlike the other tourists, we were on our way to be on the show. When we approached the front, we saw a line of people waiting to get in. It was early, so we figured we would get in line and then, once inside, let the people know why we were there. After waiting in line a few minutes, Heather advised me to go tell security who we were and see if we were in the right line. I walked up to the gentleman and asked if this was the line if you were on the show. He explained that if you want to be on the show in the audience, this is where you wait. I explained we were his guests on the show and not audience members. He gave me a funny look and asked my name. He let out a sigh, got on his radio, and exclaimed how he had found us and that we were in line to be in the audience. He said the producer was looking for us and was on her way down. Oops!

When the producer arrived, she laughed at what had happened and immediately led us inside and through security. We were taken up an elevator and into a narrow hall where there were three or four dressing rooms, also known as green rooms. Our names were on one of the doors…pinch me moment! We looked at the rest of the doors to see who the other guests were. To our left was actress Kate Bosworth, and to the right was Tarana Burke, the founder of the "Me Too" women's movement. Those ladies deserved to be there, and then there was us. Our green room was small, but it had a table of food and drinks for us to enjoy while we waited. We had a TV that showed the soundstage and what was currently being taped. After a bit, the producer came into our room to review the script and make sure we knew what we would say and talk about. I told her there were things in our viral video that could not be said on the show due to sponsorship business. The producer eased our nerves with her sweet demeanor. She then told us we were due in hair and makeup and led us to where we needed to be.

My stylist made me feel comfortable with her humor and kindness. She asked why we were the *Baseball Card Kidney Couple,* which is how they had us listed on their call sheet and schedule, so she was quite curious. After I shared our story with her, she cried out, "Oh! I know who you all are. I have seen that video!" Wow, how crazy that she knew who we were. At the same time, Heather was getting pampered like a queen, by her amazing hairstylist. She cracked me up when she asked him if she could take him home. With Heather's natural beauty, it does not take much to fix her up, and that day was no different. What the stylist team had done to her hair and makeup had her looking gorgeous. It took them longer to get me ready because I needed a lot of work done on my face. They were nitpicking every little thing to get me "camera ready" as they called it. About forty-five minutes later, we shared our appreciation with everybody and headed back to our green room. This silence *in between* times gave me ample opportunity to allow my nerves to kick in. When I was a little kid, my little brother, Chris and I pretended to be actors on a talk show discussing the movie we were in. If I could go back in time to tell myself that one day it would happen, that kid's mind would have been blown. After an unmeasurable amount of pacing, the door opened, and the producer said they were ready for us.

We were led to the same elevator as before but stopped on a different floor where the entrance to the set was. The doors opened to what sounded like a party. We could hear music and the audience clapping and cheering. We turned the corner, and our eyes widened as we glared in disbelief at the amazing ensemble. The audience filled every seat, and the electrifying energy zapped through our bodies like a bolt of lightning. The house band was playing music while the audience clapped along. Then my eyes locked on him: Harry Connick, Jr., in a blue suit. My face flushed and the knots in my stomach began to flip. Numerous cameras surrounded the set facing the couches. The makeup lady did one last magical touch-up on us and then the producer smiled and blurted, "Oh, by the way, Harry usually goes off script. Have fun!" What? Do you mean we spent all that time preparing, studying the script, and losing sleep over it, just to be told at the last second Harry does not usually use it? Then with her headphones on, she waved us onto the set, "Go, go, go!" Harry turned to look at us, and with a huge smile, he walked towards us.

As we met, he reached over and hugged Heather and told her how beautiful she looked. I then stuck my hand out for a handshake, but he said, "Get in here!" and hugged me as well. He then said something we never dreamed we would hear. Harry said to us, "I have wanted to meet you all for a long while now. Ever since I saw your video, I knew I wanted to meet you." He was excited to meet us. Wasn't it supposed to be the other way around? His down-to-earth kindness washed away all barriers and put us at ease. He led us over to the couches; we took our places and began chatting with Harry once again since we were in between cameras rolling. We talked about the trip to New York City and how we had been treated like royalty. Harry then explained they were going to show the audience our video and after that, it was go time. As I sat there looking out at the audience, I knew they were trying to figure out who we were and why we were on the show.

The director of the show stepped out and looked at us, and then began to count down on his fingers. As he got to one, he pointed to Harry. Harry began telling the audience that back in September, we had been on his show via Skype, but he wanted to re-introduce us.

He then explained how Heather had donated her kidney to me and saved my life and the video shows the moment she told me. The set had a large screen on the ground facing up towards us, so we could see what the audience and people watching on TV were seeing, and at that time it was our video. We sat there watching the audience watch it. I will never forget looking out and seeing so many people reacting to our video with gestures of realizing they indeed knew who we were. Amazing yet surreal. The audience heard Heather laugh in the video as I read the line, "Steve has struck out in life," and they also chuckled as she proclaimed it to be a baseball pun. After the clip ended, Harry proceeded to tell the audience how it made him cry again, and then he introduced us. The unexpected loudness from all of the cheering for us caught us off guard and moved us deep into the depths of our souls. They were most definitely cheering for Heather for her selfless gift, and for that, I do not blame them.

Harry said how he wished his producers had not made him watch our video again due to the emotions welling up inside. Then he turned to me and asked the very first question, "First of all, how are you feeling?" He was off script from the get-go. I responded, "Pretty darn good," and the off-script conversation continued. Harry then told us and the audience that our story was the most incredible love story, and his exact words were, "It is like the greatest story of all time." We know he did not mean it was the greatest story of all time for him, but the fact that he said it meant so much to us. After they were done taping our segment, we had some time to sit with Harry on the couch and talk and had the most genuine conversation about love, marriage, and what it should mean. Harry told Heather and me that he had experienced hardship as he watched his spouse, Jill Goodacre, go through breast cancer. He and Heather connected on that. Then Harry looked at me and pointed to his wedding ring and said, "This is the most important thing a man should own." We discussed how men need to make sure they take their marriage seriously, with love and intent, and to always be there for one another as Heather was for me.

After Harry shared his heartfelt thoughts with us about his beliefs, the three of us stood up for the CBS photographers to get some photos of us together. This once-in-a-lifetime chance was as close as we will probably ever come to walking a red carpet. After the brief photo shoot, we were led off the set as we heard the kindest remarks from audience members trying to get our attention. I felt compelled to stop and wave and say hi to a few people who said the sweetest things about us. Heather and I went back to our green room, where we had to sign some papers, and then, just like that, the enchanted TV appearance we had been anticipating for weeks came to an end. We walked back down to the lobby and out the front door and saw at least twenty paparazzi standing there. We knew they were not there for us, but rather for Kate Bosworth, which made complete sense. It was fun to imagine for a few seconds they were waiting for us, but then we laughed at ourselves over the notion and went on our way.

Chapter 32

By Steve

A TREATMENT, NOT A CURE

I had been told that life directly after a transplant can be tricky and getting admitted back into a hospital was not abnormal. This happened to me a few times, and I admit it somewhat set me back a bit, mentally. I assumed the transplant would lead me away from hospitals, but I learned all too soon that issues can still arise. A kidney transplant is not a cure…it's a treatment. When someone has kidney disease, it means something in their body is attacking the kidneys. The disease can either be a result of acute damage or genetic. Since your genetics do not change, when you receive a transplanted kidney, whatever had been attacking your kidneys will eventually come after the new one. This is why many transplant recipients end up needing more than one transplant. You must take antirejection medicine to try to ensure your body does not reject the new kidney. It is a foreign object in your body, and when a foreign object invades your body, it immediately tries to reject it or get rid of it. I will be on antirejection medications for the rest of my life, but that is a small downside compared to dialysis. It can be tricky dialing in dosages and figuring out which medications work the best. The transplant team sometimes has to experiment like you would with cooking instructions. There has to be just the right amount of each medicine for each person's body. During these times, you may need to be hospitalized if rejection begins due to an imperfect recipe of pills.

For your body to stand down and not attack your new kidney, the antirejection meds disguise the new kidney in a way that fools the white blood cells in our body to not see it as a threat. Well, the white blood cells need to be alert and ready to help your body at all times, but when you put a so-called spell on them to put them to sleep as the medicine does, this makes your body vulnerable to other infections since they are also not seen as a threat. Transplant patients are known to become sick much easier than someone who isn't taking antirejection medications, and even the common cold can escalate into something life-threatening. This has happened to me; I would catch a cold, and within a day or two those mild symptoms would advance into pneumonia since my white blood cells were not capable of attacking and fighting it off. Even though I understand why I need to take these medications, it still frustrates me when I need to be hospitalized since I had thought I closed the door on that part of my life.

Many people see transplants as a cure and that all issues, both physical and mental, suddenly disappear. Yes, a transplant is a blessing and can be life-changing, but it does not instantly fix things. Imagine being sick your entire adult life. Friends leave you in the dust, perhaps because they feel uncomfortable with your being sick all the time. Who knows why people seem to run away from a chronically ill person, but I assure you, losing those friendships hits deep in the gut. If you've read the previous chapters, you know I was that sick guy who didn't always look sick, and the guy who had to replace his career with dialysis treatment. A once-blooming career turned into finding any kind of work that could revolve around your illness schedule.

Imagine a person is sent to prison as an 18-year-old. He or she spends their entire adulthood as an inmate and soon that way of life becomes all they know. They have the same day-to-day schedule with certain expectations, and they lose connection with society and the person they used to be. Now, after a 14-year sentence, the prisoner is released...free to go. They step outside, take a deep breath, and then ask, "Now what?" Society sees them as an ex-con, and they have lost their place in the community. This person hasn't worked in years, so who would want to hire them? It's a similar situation with a chronically ill patient. Being set free is a wonderful and beautiful blessing, but then the mental pretzel of emotions that comes along with it can be deflating. Where does the sick person fit back into society? I knew I had received the greatest gift of life, but I also had no idea who I was meant to be, and where I was meant to go after my transplant.

With a new lease on life after the transplant, I wanted to do something meaningful with my existence. Helping others has always been important to me, and I was finally had the mindset to do that instead of being swallowed up by my issues. The time had come to make my life matter. I felt a nudge at my heart that I should use my survival, and the platform that came with it, to help other kidney patients. My journey had been filled with all sorts of obstacles and struggles, entwined with anger, sadness, depression, and anxiety, but I survived. The many blessings in my life, including my wife and foster kids, and finding some purpose from our viral video, countered some of the ugly. People around the world who had reached out to us gave us compliments for being so strong, but they had no idea who was hiding behind the faces they saw. Hardly anyone knew what had happened leading up to the moment in our video. They didn't see the tears of pain and hurt, or know how lost I felt for years. Social media does a great job of disguising reality with smoke and mirrors, which it did for the people watching the miracle God gave us with the kidney match and the happy tears. They only witnessed the good, but not the bad and the ugly. No one knew how often I found myself angry with God and asking why He had forgotten me. Begging on my knees for answered prayers. I just couldn't see, through the foggy lenses of my pain, that God had never left me the entire time. He was at my side through every hurt and miserable minute, and He still loved me when I questioned Him.

One of the times I felt ill after the transplant, I called the team at Vanderbilt and explained I had a fever and didn't feel like myself.

They advised me to go to the local emergency room to get checked out. I thought my frequent flier card had expired, but there I was again, back in the hospital that had almost become a second home to me, in that same building where a botched biopsy led me to need a lifesaving operation to stop the internal bleeding when I was only 18, and the same place I had my first dialysis treatment at the age of 30. The emergency room team examined me and said they were admitting me for further testing and evaluation by their nephrologist. Oh, great, another nephrologist who did not know me or my history would try to solve my unique puzzle. The hospital was the absolute last place I wanted to be. Heather wasn't with me so I let her know a nephrologist was coming to see me since my kidney numbers were off.

Finally, I heard a knock on the door, and a man called out, "Mr. Winfree!" My startled face gave away the shock I was experiencing seeing the same doctor who broke the news to me, almost twenty years ago, that I had kidney failure – Dr. Newman. We had lost touch since I moved away after graduating college, but all these years later unknown kidney issues brought us together. My mind drifted for a second as I thought back to how tough it must have been for him to tell an 18-year-old that his dream of playing college basketball was over. He told me he had heard I received a kidney transplant but was not sure if it was from a living kidney donor. He did not know my wife had donated, so that news thrilled him, and he was over the moon for me. We talked and reminisced about the day he told me I had kidney failure, having no idea of the chain of events that would follow. He remembered how scared I looked as a teenager receiving that sort of news, and he admitted how it shook him deep down to deliver that life sentence when he was trying to comprehend how it could be possible. Dr. Newman had no idea about the constant pain I experienced from gout, depression, anxiety, the hospital stays, operations, and how incredibly difficult the disease made my life. He knew nothing about me living out my dreams as an actor in Florida and then having those dreams crushed by dialysis, or the relationships that had fizzled due to the disease.

Dr. Newman walked over to me, put his hand on my left shoulder just as he did twenty years ago, and without skipping a beat he told me, "See? I told you that you would be fine."

By Heather

A SECOND CHANCE AT LIFE

The term "second chance at life" is often used in connection with organ transplantation and refers to the recipient of that gift of life. However, I feel that by gifting my left kidney to my husband, I was also given a second chance. Not just a fresh start with Steve but a new beginning myself. Maybe it is one of those things you can only be cognizant of by going through it, but I will do my best to put it into words.

Before donating my kidney, I did not consider myself a brave person. Nothing could have persuaded me to speak publicly in front of a big group of strangers. It terrified me to think about putting myself out there, or to write a book other than a personal journal. I never imagined anyone would ever want to read something about me and my life, and never in a million years would I have ever thought I would give a keynote speech in front of a room full of people smarter than myself.

Since donating a kidney, I experienced a shift. I realized I could do things that intimidated me. I could take risks and reap the immeasurable rewards. I could be brave and bold and break free from the everyday grind. Outside-of-the-box thinking and doing scared me before my donation, but my bravery gave me the courage to speak up and advocate for others. I realized I could make a difference in the world, and my decisions could inspire a positive ripple effect far greater than myself. My dreams didn't feel like just dreams anymore. My path could be unique, and I didn't have to be who everyone else expected me to be. I unapologetically felt proud to be me and live life to the fullest and how I wanted to. The gift of life I carried and gave away ignited a new passion for life in me.

After our story went viral, Representative John J. Duncan Jr. did a tribute to Steve and me in the House of Representatives. Our love story will forever be a part of American History etched into the Congressional Record of the United States of America. I cannot say how humbling it is that something I did, and something my husband and I went through, was note-worthy enough to be spoken about on such a monumental platform. Below is the Tribute:

TRIBUTE TO STEVE AND HEATHER WINFREE; Congressional Record Vol. 163, No. 121
HON. JOHN J. DUNCAN, JR.
of tennessee
in the house of representatives
Tuesday, July 18, 2017

Mr. DUNCAN of Tennessee. Mr. Speaker, heroes come into lives in different ways through the challenges people face during their lives.
A very special hero from my district came up with a heartwarming way to share her choice to be an organ donor for her husband who has been suffering from kidney disease for 14 years.
Heather Winfree took her husband's love for baseball and used it as a way to share the good news that she was a donor match.
Because of his diagnosis as a teen, Steve Winfree was never able to achieve his dream of playing college baseball.
Steve collects baseball cards on a regular basis, but the most rare card he has ever

received is a custom Topps card that Heather designed for him.

It included Steve's picture and text on the back that read "Steve will be a rookie recipient at Vanderbilt Transplant Center where his wife, Heather, will be pitching a new kidney to him."

Because of Heather's heroic efforts to save the life of her husband, he could receive the transplant as soon as the end of July this year.

I am proud to see people from my district like Heather show us the true meaning of love while people like Steve show us what perseverance looks like.

Please join me in wishing them the best as they both undergo surgery in the near future.

I would like to include in the Record the following story about the Winfrees from CBS News.

[From CBS News, July 11, 2017]

Man Learns Wife Is Kidney Transplant Match From a Custom-Made Baseball Card

(By Jennifer Earl)

Steve Winfree was excited to rip open up a brand new pack of Topps baseball cards. It has become a family tradition over the years. But this time, as he shuffled through the deck, he spotted something unusual—his very own playing card.

As he read the stats on the back, Winfree, who has been suffering from kidney disease for the past 14 years, broke down in tears.

"What the heck?" he asked, as his wife, Heather, sat beside him.

"What is it?" Heather asked, grinning.

Winfree began to read out loud: "Steve has had a lot on his plate. With his health issues, he's been striking out a lot. He was not sure how he was going to wind up," the card's bio said. "His wife, Heather, thinks he's a great catch so she's just dying to go to bat for him. Now Steve will be a rookie recipient."

It was at that moment, Winfree realized his wife was giving him the best gift of all-a new kidney, and a whole new life.

Heather Winfree surprised her husband, Steve, with his very own Topps playing card.

Heather had been tested to see if she could be a match a week earlier. Before she even received the results, she came up with the creative way to share the good news.

"I had already started planning how I was going to tell him before I knew I was a match," Heather told CBS News. "I never considered I wouldn't be a match. I guess I had to have faith I was going to be a match-that was keeping my hope alive."

Steve Winfree was diagnosed with chronic kidney disease at the age of 18. He was getting ready to play college basketball when doctors discovered he had high blood pressure during a pre-season physical.

After running more tests, Winfree was told he only had 50 percent kidney function. His dreams of playing college ball were over.

"He's been through a lot," Heather said. "Kidney disease is really hard. It's been really hard."

Since the couple met seven years ago, he's developed severe gout, arthritis, undergone several surgeries and had to have a toe amputated. He's been on dialysis for over a year.

"A year ago, they put a port in his chest and he ended up going into septic shock," Heather added. "He spent seven days in the intensive care unit. I can't tell you what that grief felt like, feeling like I was going to lose my husband."

Steve Winfree is told his wife is a perfect match for a kidney transplant, and he could have surgery as early as the end of July.

So when doctors at Vanderbilt University Medical Center told Winfree he was eligible to get onto the transplant list in late June, Heather jumped at the opportunity to offer herself up as a living kidney donor.

"I said, 'I want to expedite this. I want to help my husband get better,'" she explained.

Her wish came true when doctors confirmed the match. If everything goes well, Winfree could have surgery by the end of the month.

"Here I am, I have two kidneys and he needs one—why wouldn't I improve his quality of life?" Heather said. "For 14 years of his life he's been battling this disease and finally we have the relief of knowing the end is on the horizon. We've got hope."

About a year after that tribute was given, Steve and I travelled to Washington D.C. as advocates with the American Kidney Fund organization. I was invited to speak at a Congressional Briefing on Capitol Hill on World Kidney and International Women's Day in 2018. Since World Kidney Day and International Women's Day happened to align that year the theme of the briefing was *Women and Kidney Disease*. That day I shared my story in front of a room full of State Representatives and staff members advocating for Living Kidney Donor Rights. I pled with them to pass the Living Donor Protection Act, so donors are protected from discrimination from their employer and insurance companies related to their choice to be a living donor. Speaking in front of a room filled with people was something I never would have imagined myself doing prior to donating but there I was with a captive audience.

Once I had recovered from surgery, and felt this newfound zeal for life, I started applying for new jobs. I felt compelled to make a change and not sit stagnant and feeling unfulfilled. My newfound tenacity landed me a dream job that came with an incredible boss and a team of coworkers I enjoyed being around. My mentor at that new job knew I loved working there, but he felt obligated to warn me that the industry was notorious for layoffs. This man was an older gentleman and often joked about being bought and sold in his career more times than he could count. It only took a year for it happened to me. A merger took place with my company, and since I was the low man on the totem pole, my position was eliminated in the first wave of layoffs.

I had a gut feeling about it, and my premonition proved correct when I received an email while working late one night, wrapping up some tasks. The email was a meeting invite for first thing the next morning from my boss' boss. I knew the meeting meant my demise. Thankfully, I wasn't blindsided because of the warning my mentor had given me, so I stayed a little later to clear out my desk drawers and clean up my workspace. I brought a handful of items home with me that evening anticipating what was coming the next morning.

I walked into the conference room first thing the next morning. My boss' boss sat at the table with two people from human resources that I had never seen before, along with two other women I had worked closely with over the last year and who had come to be friends of mine. The uncomfortable conversation began, and I remember silently watching the expressions of everyone else. Across from me were the two ladies I had worked with – they were also getting laid off, and at the ends of the conference table were the people from HR along with the woman who had hired me just a year ago.

The two ladies getting laid off alongside me, unlike myself, were caught completely off guard. One of the women was older and had come over during another merger around the same time they hired me. The other woman had dedicated her whole career to that point, twenty years or so, to this company. The older woman became angry and distraught, while the other woman was devastated and felt incredibly betrayed. The human resource representatives allowed us to ask questions and vent. The other two ladies vented and the older one asked how she was supposed to provide for her disabled husband. She asked who would hire a woman of her age. I empathized with her fear and burden of how she was supposed to pick up the pieces. The other woman stood there in shock, shaking. Her voice and her whole body seemed to reflect the state of how broken she felt. My heart broke for them both. Then my boss' boss asked me if I had anything to say, and I declined. Not saying anything seemed more disconcerting to the human resource representatives and my boss' boss than the emotional responses of the other women.

What was there to say though? Nothing in this space. I knew I couldn't change their minds. The only option was to hold my head high and move forward. My husband could be a sounding board once I got home. I gave them a year of service, and the older woman gave them twenty years, but they gave us 30 minutes to gather our things and leave. The rest of the employees were segregated in another part of the office to allow us space. The woman who had been there twenty years broke down, not knowing how she could pack everything in only 30 minutes since she had accumulated so much over the years. They agreed to help her pack as much as she could in that half hour and said they would arrange for someone to come after hours that evening and help her finish.

I quickly packed my things and then asked her how I could help. We took a few trips down to her car, handed in our badges, and left the office. I called Steve from the parking garage to let him know my gut feeling had been correct. He had tried to reassure me the night before not to worry, but it still caught him off guard when I called to say I was on my way home. My best friend and husband gave me what I needed on that drive home; an ear to vent to about losing the job I loved, but all I could do was sob and say, "Those poor women." I explained to Steve what I had just witnessed and how my heart broke for them. Even though I was in the same seat as them, I felt more empathy for them than I did for myself.

I knew deep down that I could rebound from this. Over the next few days and amidst a little panic, I sent out a ton of applications and résumés. Those efforts produced a lot of interviews over the next few weeks, which turned on a light bulb in my head...it occurred to me that maybe this loss was, in fact, a blessing. I had received a small severance package from the company, but a severance, nonetheless, which I was grateful for. Steve encouraged me to take time to think about what I genuinely wanted to do with my professional life. After thought and prayer, it came to me – I wanted to help people.

I found a program with AmeriCorps VISTA, which is like the Peace Corps but here in America. AmeriCorps members volunteer with local nonprofits to help tackle the nation's most pressing challenges. I applied for a local summer program that involved helping children. These volunteer positions pay a small stipend, plus an education voucher that goes toward any student loans you might have. The stipend would help supplement my severance pay, allow me time to think about what I wanted to do next, and give me a much-needed break from the corporate world. I looked forward to serving my community and taking a step back from the day-to-day grind of office work. The program they selected me for meant I would get to spend the summer days ahead with children.

For my position, I traveled throughout my county to several housing project locations every day to help feed food insecure children. The experience turned out to be more incredible than I had imagined! Every morning, we would meet at a local high school, load up our van with lunches, and then head out to several projects throughout the community, handing out lunches and sitting with these children. Sometimes we ate outside picnic-style under the trees, and sometimes in their community centers or at parks nearby. This new perspective of life humbled me, and feelings of self-pity I had disappeared. The simplicity of children showing gratitude for a meal made me incredibly grateful for all I had.

That summer flew by like a swift breeze, but I was not ready to step away from serving children in my community. Their light and laughter were renewing my spirit in ways I had no idea I needed. The fulfilling work I did that summer inspired me to continue in that field, and I found a job posting for a preschool teacher working with children who had been exposed to drugs in utero. This preschool program was located at an outpatient facility that helped mothers who were recovering addicts. While the mothers attended classes and therapy, their children would also be enriched with love and learning onsite. I had no experience teaching, but I knew I had a heart for those mothers and their babies. The director reached out for an interview, and I remember her telling me that my gentleness was a strength they needed in their program.

Until then, I had never heard of or even considered my gentleness as a strength. It had always been an obstacle in my previous occupation. I remember being criticized, one time during a performance review at a previous job, for not being aggressive enough. Gentleness sounded much more appealing than needing to be aggressive, so I gladly accepted the position for the interim, not sure how I would pay the bills in the long term. The routine of the day at the preschool comforted me, and the little lives I nourished, nourished my soul in return.

A few months into my teaching venture, I received a phone call from the director of the VISTA program I had been a part of. He remembered my prior work had been in finance, and he had been contacted by a former AmeriCorps VISTA who worked for the State of Tennessee in finance. They wanted to see if any recent AmeriCorps VISTAs had come through with a financial background. He immediately thought of me, so I applied for the position and got it. My heart broke to say goodbye to my teaching position, but the new chapter ahead of me exhilarated me.

Chapter 34

By Heather & Steve

"LOVE IS THE MOST IMPORTANT THING IN THE WORLD, BUT BASEBALL IS PRETTY GOOD, TOO"

-YOGI BERRA

Heather

My time spent working with kids reinforced my desire to have children of my own. Steve and I attended an Atlanta Braves game in April of 2021 with some friends, and on the drive home, I downloaded a book on my Kindle app about embryo donation /adoption. A friend had told me about it several years before, but something sparked my looking into it on that drive home. Before I even finished reading the first chapter, I told Steve I wanted to read this book with him. The entire drive home, I read the book aloud, and throughout the following month, I dove deeper into researching more about embryo donation.

Here is a summary of embryo donation:

First, we have to understand what IVF (invitro fertilization) is: IVF is a procedure where eggs are retrieved from the ovaries and then fertilized outside of the womb to create embryos. This procedure is often used by couples who are struggling to conceive for a lot of different reasons including male factor infertility, damaged fallopian tubes, unexplained infertility, and other reasons.

Once the eggs are retrieved and fertilized by the sperm, the doctor can perform a fresh transfer using one or more embryos, transferring them to the uterus using a catheter through the cervix. Or the doctor can freeze the embryos and then thaw and transfer at a later time. In some cases, a couple will complete their family and still have some frozen embryos remaining.

There are a few options of what to do with the remaining embryos: they can be stored indefinitely (as long as the couple continues to pay storage fees to the clinic where they are frozen), they can be donated to science to improve treatment options for future patients or stem cell research, they can be discarded, or they can be donated to another person or couple so they can grow their family.

Steve

I remember we were coming home from an Atlanta Braves game, and Heather brought up the idea of embryo donation. I had never heard of it before, but she seemed very intrigued and excited about it, so I became intrigued myself. She read this article about "snowflake babies," how families that had completed their family through assistive reproduction had remaining frozen embryos, and they could give those embryos a chance at life by donating them to another family struggling to conceive.

I had never heard of this before, but it sounded as if it was a viable option for us. When Heather becomes interested in something, she does a wonderful job of researching every aspect of it, so when she first approached me about this, I could tell she had been thinking about this for some time. She asked me how I felt about becoming a dad and watching her give birth to a child that was not genetically mine. This was a very deep question and clearly something I had never thought about before. I took my time as I answered, and I brought up how my heart belonged to children, six as a matter of fact, who were not carrying a single ounce of my DNA – our former foster children. I knew what it felt like to love a child that was not "mine," so I explained how this would be no different.

We prayed about this monumental decision for our family, and at the end of the day, we knew it was something we wanted to officially explore. Although there were odds against us in regard to the transfer working, we knew we wanted to try. Every embryo deserves the opportunity to live, and we wanted to do what we could to find the right embryos. I understood my main role in this process was emotional support and to be there with Heather every step of the way. I was determined to love her through this as though the baby was genetically mine.

Chapter 35

By Heather & Steve

THE END?

Heather

Through my research and conversations with Steve, I decided the best outcome for our family would be to find a family who would directly donate to us so that we (and any resulting children) could have a relationship with our donor/our child's genetic family. First, I needed to become an established patient at a fertility clinic that would accept donated embryos from another clinic. I learned that a lot of clinics will not accept embryos created at another clinic because they cannot guarantee the quality of the procedures used during the process. I made a post introducing myself to an embryo donation group I had found on Facebook. The post said a little bit about Steve and me, and that I was there to learn about the process. What happened next surpassed anything I could have imagined and filled me with so much hope. I received so many encouraging messages and then one that simply said, "Please feel free to message me. My partner and I have some remaining frozen embryos. We have a wonderful child, but we have got to decide what to do with them." I sent them a message.

"I am not sure what all to share or what to ask. Please share only what you feel comfortable with. What are your hopes for you and your partners' remaining embryos? Are you planning on having any more children? Do you want contact with potential children from your embryos? If so, what do you imagine that would look like?

A little about my husband and me: we have been married for nine years. I have always wanted to be a mom! We were foster parents for four years to six incredible kids, ages newborn to 10 years old, but we were unable to adopt them. Two of the children we fostered are now with their biological grandma, and we have been able to stay in contact with them. We are their godparents now. We live in Tennessee and would want our children to always know where they came from, and ideally, we are looking for some type of relationship with our donors. I would love to hear more about you and your partner when you get the chance."

That message then turned into a phone conversation, and we talked for a little over an hour getting to know each other. We laughed about how weird the situation felt, but we also connected on how we valued life. The call ended on a positive note, and we would touch base after we all had more to think and pray about this. A week later I received a phone call asking if we would like to adopt their embryos. I could not believe how easy it turned out to be. Do not get me wrong, it also felt complicated at times. There was a lot of thought and emotions that went into making this decision on both our end and our donor's end, but it just felt so right from the beginning.

The next step in the process was paperwork to get the embryos transferred over into our names, and then I had to arrange to have the embryos moved to our clinic. This took a little bit of coordinating because our embryos were in California, and we were in Tennessee. Believe it or not, some companies specialize in the transportation of cryopreserved (frozen) embryos. This jabbed at my nerves because I was afraid of something happening to these precious little embryos during transportation. They ended up taking a plane ride from California to Tennessee and then were transported to our clinic. The transport company kept in contact throughout the process with delivery updates. The relief I felt when I received notification that our embryos arrived safely at the clinic, I'm sure was the same as any mother knowing her child made it safely to their destination.

Now we had to begin the process of getting my body ready for a transfer. That included multiple appointments, some medications, and a lot of ultrasounds to ensure the embryo was transferred at exactly the right time. They scheduled my transfer day for Labor Day, 2021. If the transfer was successful, I would be laboring in about nine months! The clinic explained to us that the embryologist would start the thawing process that morning, and if, for some reason, the embryo did not survive the thaw, they would call to get my permission before thawing another one. As we got ourselves ready that morning, we did not receive a call so no news was good news. I found it difficult to contain my anticipation as we drove to the clinic, but my nerves assisted with that.

The process went much easier than I expected. Steve held my hand as a nurse maneuvered an ultrasound Doppler on my belly looking at my uterus. The embryologist confirmed my name and birthdate and then verified she was handing off the correct embryo to the doctor. Then the doctor inserted the catheter through my vagina and up the cervix, and the embryo was implanted on my uterus wall. It all happened so fast. Steve and I watched the ultrasound monitor and saw as the embryo was placed in my womb. An amazing sight! Our fertility doctor, knowing our story, made a joke about how it was a little easier than a kidney transplant. Then came the hard part… waiting.

It is hard to determine, based on symptoms alone, if you are pregnant when you conceive using assisted reproduction because you are taking medications that have side effects resembling pregnancy. My only out-of-the-ordinary symptom was I had the hiccups a few days after the transfer. I did not have the patience to wait, so I took a pregnancy test five days after the transfer. Were my eyes deceiving me, or were there two lines? I did not believe it. On day six I took another test. Was I seeing two lines again? Still disbelief. On day seven…yep, I took another test. No doubt there was definitely a second line. I still could not believe it. I had never seen two lines in my life on any pregnancy test I ever took. I needed to hear confirmation from the doctor that I was pregnant before I would believe it.

Steve and I were instructed to go to a local lab to get my blood drawn, and the lab was told to send the results to our clinic STAT. We were on the doorstep of the lab as soon as they opened at 7 a.m. We then waited for the clinic to call us with the results. I could not concentrate all day. The clinic called early afternoon to tell us they had not received the results yet but would call when they did. Then we got another call at 6:45 p.m. from the clinic apologizing, but they had still not gotten the results, so we would not know anything until the next day. Steve and I were emotionally exhausted from the rollercoaster ride of phone calls so we decided to go out for a bite to eat. While we were at dinner, I saw on my phone that I had received an email from the lab saying my results had been uploaded to my portal. Steve and I decided to wait until we got home to open the results. We did not want to make a scene at the restaurant, especially since my emotions were all over the place.

I prayed to see an HCG level of over 100, which would indicate I was four weeks pregnant.

The HCG read 139.

I was pregnant!

The transfer worked. We were going to have a baby. I was going to be a mother. My dreams were coming true.

Steve

When it was time to check the results of her test and HCG levels, we decided to go to the one special place where good news had been welcomed before – our front porch swing. We also wanted to get the moment on camera as an incredible memory if we indeed found out she was pregnant. Butterflies twirled in my stomach, and my heart raced a hundred miles an hour as we awaited the big moment.

With the camera set up and the moment upon us, I hit play and made my way to the swing. Heather had her phone out, and she began to slowly click and scroll down to see the results. In what took a split second seemed like five minutes. My breath left my lungs as I awaited her reaction to the results. Heather began to cry as she exclaimed, "Oh, my goodness, I'm pregnant! We have a number over 100 – I am four weeks pregnant!"

Seeing my wife become impregnated through embryo donation was amazing but also foreign to me. It was not the usual way of going about becoming a father, but I was thrilled to see my wife have her dreams come true. After everything she had done for me, she deserved this moment so much. I could not help but cry as I watched her, once again, crying on the porch swing because a dream, a goal she set out to accomplish despite the odds, had come true for her.

I have always carried a level of guilt for not being able to help Heather achieve her dream of becoming pregnant. This is the woman I would do anything for, yet I was completely helpless in this scenario. I was very open to the idea when she first mentioned looking into an embryo transfer, and I was determined to see her become pregnant.

The only children we had up to this point were foster children, so loving a child who was not genetically ours was a very easy thing to do. Every child deserves love, and no matter how we came about being parents, I was going to love that child more than anything. I was going to give my entire heart to that child and be a real dad. I never thought I would see the day when I would get to be a father and see my wife give birth, but if there is one thing I have learned from my story, it is when you feel like life is down to nothing, God is up to something. Never stop believing and always remain strong in your faith. I was alive and married to my soulmate, and together we were going to be parents to a beautiful baby.

Heather

I wouldn't say my pregnancy went off without a hitch, but it was still truly magical. I loved being pregnant despite some difficulties. I dealt with pain, exhaustion, and then gestational hypertension and gestational diabetes late in my pregnancy. Even on the most difficult days though, I savored it all. I treasured every milestone – hearing the heartbeat for the first time, the first kick, my belly growing bigger, and finding out I was having a baby boy. It still did not feel real though. Until I held him, I do not think I would let myself believe it.

At last, our little one's birthday arrived. My doctor scheduled a C-section due to my gestational hypertension and because the baby was not in a good position to be delivered vaginally. We had to check into the hospital at 6:00 a.m. Our early morning drive brought me back to the kidney transplant and the unspoken words we didn't need to say on the drive to Vanderbilt. I knew Steve was on edge more than me. Unlike the transplant experience, once we were at the hospital things moved fast. Before I even had a chance to get the jitters, they were wheeling me into the operating room. As instructed, I scooted off the bed and onto the operating table, and then they positioned me sitting up with my legs dangling off the bed. The anesthesiologist stood behind me, and a nurse was in front of me for moral support and to help keep me as still and calm as possible while the anesthesiologist placed the epidural in my spine. The nurse held my hands and encouraged me the whole time. It was uncomfortable but it did not last long.

Shortly after, they let Steve come in. He couldn't come in at the beginning due to the hospital not letting the birthing partner be there during the epidural. They have this protocol in place because the needle is so big, and they do not want the partner to pass out. They got Steve a chair and had him sit near my head. Then they prepped me for the C-section and hung a curtain between me and my belly. I could not believe how excited I felt, but this was what I had wanted almost my entire life. My husband was right there by my side, so sweet and encouraging. Steve told me how beautiful I looked, and how proud he was of me, and that he knew I would be a wonderful mom to our baby.

Within no time our son made his entrance into the world. The team brought him over to the scale to be weighed and wiped off, and then they wrapped him in a blanket and placed a tiny pink and blue striped hat on his head. The nurse handed our baby to Steve and he carried him over to me and placed him on my chest. Our child, our miracle, was the most beautiful child I had ever seen. Love at first sight. I kissed his little cheek and told him over and over how much I loved him. I sobbed tears of joy as I experienced a love I had never experienced before. Then I heard my doctor say, "Heather, I am going to ask an impossible task from you, ok?"

Through the tears, I replied, "Yeah."

He said, "I need you to try to stop crying for just a minute."

My uncontrolled crying was making it difficult for him to sew me back up. I had tuned everything and everyone out, other than Steve, myself, and our precious baby at that moment. We were in our own little magical world. Somehow, I stopped sobbing so the doctor could finish his job, and I marveled at the little human I held in my arms. God had bestowed his greatest blessing upon us and made me the happiest woman on earth.

I had given Steve the gift of life, and the gift of life had been given back to me.

Levi Bennett Winfree
7 pounds 2 ounces
Born 8:31 a.m.

A beautiful beginning.

KIDNEY DISEASE STATISTICS

- 37 million Americans have kidney disease
- Every 24 hours, more than 360 people begin dialysis treatment for kidney failure. Kidney disease can often be prevented, and the progression of kidney disease to kidney failure can often be slowed down or stopped.
- About 808,000 Americans are living with kidney failure
- More than 556,000 Americans are on dialysis
- More than 250,000 Americans are living with a kidney transplant
- Kidney disease is growing at an alarming rate. It currently affects more than 1 in 7—or 14%—of American adults, with people of color at greater risk for kidney failure.
- Nearly 136,000 people in the U.S. were newly diagnosed with kidney failure in 2021 (the most recent data available)
- The prevalence of kidney failure in the United States rose 24% between 2011 and 2021.
- 9 out of 10 people with kidney disease are unaware they have it, and about 1 in 3 adults with severe CKD do not know they have CKD.
- Nearly 40% of people who start on dialysis did not even know they had kidney disease.
- About 1 in 3 adults with diabetes may have kidney disease. Diabetes is the top cause of kidney failure, causing about 44% of new cases in 2021.
- 1 in 5 adults with high blood pressure may have kidney disease. High blood pressure is the second most common cause of kidney failure, causing 29% of new cases in 2021.
- There are more than 90,000 Americans on the kidney transplant waiting list, but in 2023, just 28,144—or nearly 1 in 4—were able to get a kidney. Most of these transplants were from deceased donors. There were 6,290 living donor kidney transplants performed in the U.S. last year.
- There are 1,046 children (age 17 and younger) on the kidney transplant list as of April 26, 2024.
- The shortage of available donor kidneys means that the vast majority of people who develop kidney failure are treated with dialysis. Of the 136,000 Americans newly diagnosed with kidney failure in 2021 (most recent data), nearly 97% of them began dialysis. Only 4,153 were able to receive a preemptive kidney transplant.

American Kidney Fund
KidneyFund.org
KidneyFund.org/Donate

Printed in the USA
CPSIA information can be obtained
at www.ICGtesting.com
LVHW020928150524
780224LV00016B/710